# LOVE, WARMTH, AND DISCIPLINE

# LOVE, WARMTH, AND DISCIPLINE

## LESSONS FROM BOYS TOWN FOR SUCCESSFUL PARENTING

### By Rev. Val J. Peter

Executive Director Emeritus of Boys Town

Our Sunday Visitor Publishing Division
Our Sunday Visitor, Inc.
Huntington, Indiana 46750

*Nihil Obstat:* Msgr. Michael Heintz, Ph.D.
*Censor Librorum*

*Imprimatur:* ✠ Kevin C. Rhoades
Bishop of Fort Wayne-South Bend
February 15, 2010

The *Nihil Obstat* and *Imprimatur* are official indications that a book or pamphlet is free from doctrinal or moral error. No implication is contained therein that those who have granted the *Nihil Obstat* or *Imprimatur* agree with the contents, opinions, or statements expressed.

Our Sunday Visitor Publishing Division
Our Sunday Visitor, Inc.
200 Noll Plaza
Huntington, IN 46750
1-800-348-2440
bookpermissions@osv.com

ISBN: 978-1-59276-687-1 (Inventory No. T966)
LCCN: 2009943159

Cover design: Lindsey Luken / Cover photo: Jupiter Unlimited
Interior design: Siok-Tin Sodbinow

PRINTED IN THE UNITED STATES OF AMERICA

# Contents

# Introduction

Change is sweeping across America, both in the economy and in politics, in ways we have not seen for decades. This is a book for these times. It's for moms and dads, for teachers, for youth care workers, for other church people, and for all who want to help kids in better ways than before, including politicians, lawyers, and judges.

So often today, adults are discouraged in working with young people. In many cases, they have been told too many horror stories. Way back in August of 2001, the cover of *Time* magazine asked if kids had too much power. The answer was a resounding yes!

I have dealt daily with adolescent boys and girls and their families for twenty-five years. When you do this, you learn lessons, very important lessons. These lessons are expressed here first in "text message" shorthand, then elaborated upon as "dispatches from the front" — namely, the front lines of the battle in which so many Americans engage when we deal with our children. In some ways, it's true that this is a "battle," but in many more ways, it doesn't have to be . . . and we can show you how to change it. This book is meant to help you "win the war."

So this is a book of encouragement. Moms and dads, teachers and counselors, you really can find success, joy, happiness, and fulfillment in raising your children. You just have to know a few secrets and develop a few new skills.

The legal realm today expects more from parents and helps less; your place as parent has eroded. But the good news is, it can be restored. What we have learned at Boys Town can help you. We can help youth ministers, teachers, and pastors. Each chapter describes some of these secrets of success. Please take them to heart. Please take them to prayer. Please take them to your children.

Some sociologists and psychologists are, at times, fond of reminding us that just about every generation thinks the kids are the worst ever, meaning nothing much has changed. These experts smile condescendingly and tell us that teenagers today are doing a lot of volunteer work; they tell us that they are having fewer babies, fewer abortions, and all manner of good things. Much of this is true. But what they don't talk about is that teenage life has become more toxic, coarse, and difficult in certain basic areas, and many of these aren't the same as they were in the '60s and '70s. So if any self-satisfied commentator tells you nothing much has changed, he is clearly whistling Dixie. Moms and dads, it is time to gain resilience in your lives and to help your children gain resilience in theirs.

Yes, it's time for change.

Is it possible we've learned some secrets you can use? It sure is. Here are a few stories that recent graduates from Boys Town tell about themselves. They are meant to be a source of inspiration and encouragement to you. Armed with new skills, with the grace of God and with a solid spiritual life, you and I and all of us, as families, as schools, as Church, can have more success and more joy.

———◅◦◦◦◦►———

Before I came to Boys Town, I was a troubled young boy looking for a way out. I was kicked out of school. When I came here, I wasn't expecting anyone to help me. I thought the Family-Teachers were going to be arrogant adults who abused their authority. It wasn't that way. They are great people. They have taught me and made me a mature young person. I am grateful.

— Jordan

Before I came to Boys Town, I was living a life that was leading me nowhere. I knew I would amount to nothing. I had an attitude problem. I was very selfish. It kept me from things in life that were far more important. I was doing nothing to mend my family's relationships. I didn't want to give up things in my life. I was destroying any chance to be successful. So when I came, I felt I needed something new. I didn't know what it was, but I knew something had to change in order to progress anywhere. It took me a while to learn, but I did learn and I am grateful. I am an example of what Boys Town can really do for you.

— Cameron

When I came to Boys Town, I was going nowhere fast. I was full of anger and was depressed. My anger turned to aggression at an early age. I was confrontational. I couldn't stay anywhere without getting into a fight or an argument. So when I came to Boys Town,

I was still doing the same kinds of things that didn't really click for me but, at the same time, I didn't want it to stop. I hated it here. I never gave Boys Town a chance. I should have. I was always in trouble. One day I realized that there were no Family-Teachers who wanted me in their house and, that day, I realized I didn't want to be the kid that no adult liked. So I started to change. I gave Boys Town a chance. I didn't hate it anymore and I began to like it. My grades went from C's and D's to A's and B's. I was not depressed. I was not mad at the world. You helped me change. You are my family. I had a family before, but we weren't family. Boys Town gave me a relationship with my stepmom, a relationship with my dad I never thought I would have. You set me up for success. Thank you Boys Town.

— Maria

When I came to Boys Town, I wasn't interested in getting better. I was interested in myself. I wanted what I thought I needed and everything was wrapped around me. What Boys Town has done for me is make me a different person, physically, mentally, emotionally and spiritually. I am no longer the selfish person I was. I will be a good person because of this.

— Gina

———✺———

It sounds like we are on to something.

**— Father Val J. Peter, JCD, STD**
**Executive Director Emeritus**

# CHAPTER ONE

# Where Are We and How Did We Get Here?

———◦◉◦———

*U need 2 no how parenting xperts r pedling propaganda . . . ur feeling guilty bout daring 2 disiplin is snake oil . . . don't by it . . . holesum catholic families r possible.*

You need to know how parenting experts are peddling propaganda . . . your feeling guilty about daring to discipline is snake oil . . . don't buy it . . . wholesome Catholic families are possible.

In my twenty-five years at Boys Town, I have sought root causes for the breakdown in American families in both parents and children — in their interaction, their stages of development, and the various environments in which they interact. I have looked at their churches, schools, gyms, sports, music, and the malls they cruise in. This first "dispatch from the front" shares with you what I have found.

But first, a few observations.

Survey after survey shows that one of the principal concerns of teachers is the breakdown of respect manifested by lack of safety in the classroom, chaos in the halls, and violence in the schoolyard. Bullying in grade school has become more common, and not just among boys. How did our grade schools become such places of violence? Even happy-go-lucky pre-teen boys and girls who love the high energy and choreographed routines of *High School Musical 3* undergo a cloudy, even murky, metamorphosis as they transition into junior high and high school if the parental relationships are not in balance. We should be able to expect that their childhood, if intact, gives way to new moderate troubles of adolescence, a state of affairs manageable by parents confident, firm, and warm. However, all too often, in place of these garden-variety troubles of adolescence, there is a subdural anger underpinning an over-eroticized lifestyle and a vanishing wholesomeness.

When kids come into Boys Town's residential programs from all over America, many are literally out of control. Are they that unusual? Yes, they are exaggerated artifacts. Certainly not all children are like the ones at Boys Town. In fact, perhaps only one out of every five or six youth develops some significant measure of extreme behavioral traits. But social science practitioners tell us that when about 8 percent of any population becomes unhealthy, it in turn impacts the whole population in varying degrees. And all too often, the kids we see are just a stone's throw beyond what many parents can already see developing in their own adolescents.

So let's begin by looking at the road we've traveled that has ended in unhealthy, unrewarding parenting.

During the Great Depression years, families had their distress; their dysfunctionalities; their long, almost endless, days of darkness. But although they had their tough times,

**DISPATCH A**

Juliet, a young grade-school teacher from Uganda, came to Boys Town in the summer to work with our kids and learn our youth care techniques. Her first day on the job, two of our typical out-of-control boys, ages 9 and 11, screamed, yelled, and hollered at her. Joey called her a "fat b—" and Juan called her a "f— a— b—." Juliet was shocked beyond belief. When she continued to insist on their following her instructions (as we had trained her to do), the boys threw temper tantrums (No one is going to tell me what to do!) and were very rude (Why don't you go back to Africa?), Juliet was shocked because back in Kampala, children in her classroom were bright, respectful, happy, alert, and ready to follow teachers' instructions.

they had compensations in terms of certain helpful elements that are no longer present today. The main element, almost a linchpin of success, was a non-permissive parenting culture — a balance of warmth and authority, if a shade over-authoritarian. Parents were caring and sharing in rough-hewn ways. Through a convergence of economic and social factors, parents and children shared meals, household chores, the joys of the little things they had, and the sorrows of what was beyond their reach. Family members were more dependent on each other, more intertwined.

In those days, life for many was reduced to a single narrow focus — economic survival — and no one had the luxury of going it alone. The culture wouldn't permit it. The economy wouldn't permit it. Parents wouldn't permit it. The family was a united front. Everyone had to think more of one another and rely more on one another. Kids shared the same bedrooms, bathroom, and hand-me-downs of all sorts, both tangible and intangible. There was no other way.

In those days, family structure, societal factors, and economic circumstances made us tend to look for the positive side of an arduous situation. Our only other option would have been despair. Our expectations were not sky-high. Our parents taught us what they knew. They fashioned us as best they could. They helped us grow up. That period of scarcity and physical hardship was not an idyllic time, but, in retrospect, we sometimes look upon it as a good time for the lessons it taught. We could be happy with simple things, homemade toys, and childhood games. At its best, a healthy interdependence and a fabric of warmth permeated American family life.

That fabric and that interdependence are now unraveled. But how did it happen? How did the family fabric start to slowly rip and shred after World War II?

High on the list of answers are economic and social influences. Yet another factor, very important and hardly ever noticed, also existed: a subtle, sustained, almost unconscious assault on parental authority in the aftermath of World War II.

**DISPATCH B**

Tami's 12-year-old daughter kept insisting that her mom needed to buy her a cell phone. The response to mom's repeated "No" was, "I'll tell all the kids in class you are a bad mother." Tami, a single mother, is afraid, so she gives into the threats of being reported to Child Protective Services.

The first and most obvious factor is the economic boom brought by World War II. Along with lots of jobs came social dislocation. It wasn't just that millions of men were away fighting a war; millions of women then joined the work force, leaving their children at home. After the war, women did not give up employment and careers *en masse* and return to their traditional role of homemaking. They increasingly combined the two, with both rewarding and discouraging consequences. Talcott Parsons focused on this in his book *The Social System* (unfortunately, out of print).

Many people who lived through these times can still recall the post-war boom. What is not quite so easy to recall is the slow eroding of traditional family authority. Recognized or not, the united factors of a family-centered culture, a non-affluent economy, and traditional parenting were rapidly eroding, and our thinking was being imperceptibly influenced. It seemed that affluence and change in family style went hand-in-hand. These things were welcomed and embraced, in many cases justifiably — but this, combined with the economic factors, caused the family fabric we had taken for granted to begin to fall apart. In other words, authority began slowly, ever so imperceptibly, to be pushed to the side, put in an increasingly negative light, frequently disregarded, and then even ridiculed and made fun of, especially among the more highly educated middle class. And at its beginning, there was no huge national debate about it in our churches, schools, or communities. When that national debate came about in the 1960s, it was already too late.

Let's reflect on this.

During World War II, totalitarian leaders abused legitimate authority so profoundly and pervasively that suspicion and fear began to creep into the minds of opinion makers about any and all use of authority, including the traditional family. Perhaps the seminal figure at this time was Adolph Hitler who, claiming legitimate authority, led what had been otherwise a civilized nation into a killing contest and an unthinkable Holocaust with the monumental corruption of authority in the Nazi hierarchy visible for all to behold. Japanese warlords did the same on the other side of the globe. At the war crimes trials, both in Nuremburg and Tokyo, those accused of crimes against humanity used as their defense, "We were only following orders." No wonder respect and trust for authority began to be eroded.

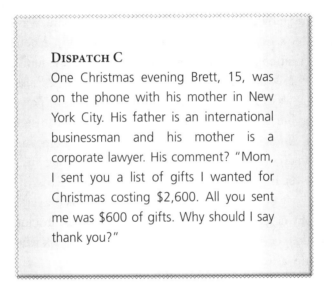

### DISPATCH C
One Christmas evening Brett, 15, was on the phone with his mother in New York City. His father is an international businessman and his mother is a corporate lawyer. His comment? "Mom, I sent you a list of gifts I wanted for Christmas costing $2,600. All you sent me was $600 of gifts. Why should I say thank you?"

(Incidentally, church authority was not included in this scrutiny at first. Respect for church authority was one of the last to be impacted because this was the realm of the sacred, an area where greater respect was due and received. But the winds of change were whistling, even at the church doors. It was only a matter of time.)

After World War II, Joseph Stalin — also claiming legitimate authority — continued and intensified a reign of terror that Aleksandr Solzhenitsyn exposed for all the world to see in *The Gulag Archipelago*. Stalin's abuse of authority was held up to ridicule by the whole free world. So, too, was Chairman Mao's abuse of authority as thousands, perhaps millions, perished in periodic famines and persecutions of enemies of the state. Then there was Pol Pot's Khmer Rouge who, in Cambodia, had the blood of at least three million on their hands (as graphically portrayed in the chilling movie *The Killing Fields)*. In the Vietnam War, our children's pride in and affection for our beloved country were shattered with the battering ram of "Hey, hey, LBJ, how many boys have you killed today?" Then, President Nixon was forced to resign due to the abuse of power in Watergate. Decades before, Lord Acton, in his insightful study *Essays in the History of Liberty,* had come to the personal conclusion that "where you have a concentration of power in a few hands, all too frequently men with the mentality of gangsters get control. History has proven that. All power corrupts; absolute power corrupts absolutely." Should it come as a surprise that some began to ask whether Acton was on to something?

In the wake of World War II (Hitler) and the Cold War (Stalin), a series of authors and childcare experts (we shall see them later) appeared on the American landscape, proclaiming that the parental discipline and firm obedience traditionally used to raise children were a major reason why such abuses of legitimate authority occurred in the Axis Powers of Germany, Japan, Italy, and elsewhere in the world. These sophisticated books, written with educated people in mind, claimed that if you raise your children with a heavy hand, they will use a heavy hand when they grow up. The solution of these authors was simple and straightforward —

parents should be therapists, not disciplinarians, and they certainly shouldn't be strict moralists.

> **DISPATCH D**
>
> On her fourteenth birthday, Gina is taken to a tattoo artist, who puts a Playboy bunny on her ankle. Her mother's comment: "You are a young woman now."

This series of economic and cultural shifts was surrounded by what we today call cultural conditioning and mass marketing by spin doctors. It was cleverly done. Totalitarian regimes stamped out the freedom of individuals and demanded from them not only external conformity (you will all do what we say) but internal conformity, too (you will all believe in your hearts Hitler makes sense and is right). In those days, it was called propaganda. Today, it is referred to as "marketing" or "environmental persuasion." Some call it the abuse of salesmanship; others say it is the abuse of advertising.

Why were the Americans of those days so easily sold this bill of goods? In the fall of 1945, the American people, utterly exhausted from a terrible war that had just ended in August, found in bookstores a new work by a Dr. Benjamin Spock, titled *Baby and Child Care*. America had dropped two atomic bombs on Japan just a few short months before its publication in 1945; Spock said his writings were motivated by the threat of nuclear war. He, like so many others, saw the horrific examples of misuse of authority in wartime — but instead of concluding that the misuse of authority was the problem, he held that *authority itself* was to blame. In this new framework, then, punishment of any kind became anathema, and parents needed to immediately abandon any punitive disciplinary practices with their children.

---

**DISPATCH E**

Savanna is a 17-year-old who, with her mother's approval, spent $600 on her 23-year-old boyfriend for his birthday in September. He is too busy playing Halo III with his friends to take her out for her October birthday.

---

Dr. Spock's work became enormously influential. With an easy, reassuring style, he taught new mothers not only about diaper rash, but also about the evils of traditional ways to raise children. He gained national attention by chastising the traditional approach of parents. He called it authoritarian, heavy-handed, unfair, and counterproductive. No hue and cry rose against him. After all, he was not attacking a new generation's parenting skills; he was just telling them not to do it the way their parents did. He was simply initiating newly married couples into the art of parenting

Dr. Spock's authority was so enormous partially because he was such a good pediatrician and partially because he was such a good propagandist. Many believed what he said: that punishment isn't healthy for a child, a mother, or any civilized people. Sad to say, a few believed (in vain) this would usher in a new era of peace. Others — the majority — simply went along with the trend.

Incidentally, most people have forgotten that by 1967, Dr. Spock gave up the practice of medicine to join the Anti-War movement. He even ran for President in 1972 on the People's Party ticket. His thesis: just as nations need to disarm, so do parents and other authority figures. Now, common sense might tell you that if parents disarm, the kids will take over, and it won't be very pretty. Look at William Golding's *Lord of the Flies* (1954). But the takeover by kids doesn't happen overnight. It is slow. It is like the high school physics experiment of the frog in lukewarm water that ends up being boiled without the frog jumping out.

Why was it so easy for one man's ideas about family life to overturn traditional practices? The answer is complex. Part of the reason was that the world was tired from war. Another was that people rejoiced in their new affluence. New parents let their guard down. Gradually, America was flooded with a series of anti-authoritarian books.

Psychoanalyst Rudolph Dreikur's *The Challenge of Parenthood* (1958) told parents to embrace democracy by having family councils. Political freedom, economic freedom and individual freedom for children and parents went hand in hand. Some parents even gave their children voting rights. The march toward a change in parenting continued with Haim Ginnott's *Between Parent and Child* (1965) and *Between Parent and Teenager* (1969). Then there was Thomas Gordon's *P.E.T. Parent Effectiveness Training* (1970). In one sense, these experts intimidated middle-class and upper middle-class moms and dads who were too afraid to practice traditional parenting with warmth and firm discipline. This and other factors transformed their families.

Over generations, common sense had told parents that if they were to help their children develop a conscience, they would have to back up their words with loving but firm authority and even lay down the law about lying, cheating, stealing, and about honoring their father and their mother. But in decrying any authority of any kind, the new "experts" made no distinction at the time between what we today call *authoritarian* parenting (harsh "spare the rod and spoil the child" approach) and *authoritative* parenting (warm and nurturing, imposing firm limits, demands, and controls). Authoritative parenting through all the centuries had been rewarded with good results — but, despite that, experts maintained that parents imposing any authority was all wrong.

And so, a *permissive parenting culture* slowly became more and more popular. The best argument against it was the hordes of out-of-control teenagers whom it did not civilize, especially amid the middle and the upper middle class. On the other hand, the permissive parenting experts argued that the "only" alternative to such an approach — beat kids into submission with a stick: namely, authoritarian parenting — was unthinkable. Once the culture and economy turned on parents who were authoritarian, physical discipline became increasingly ineffective and counterproductive.

In the late '60s and early '70s, the anti-war protests and the Civil Rights movement led to additional successful attacks on the misuse of authority — and, unfortunately, legitimate authority as well. These attacks indirectly helped to reinforce the notion that traditional parenting should be put in the dustbin of history.

By the 1980s, the problems of drugs, alcohol, and sexual promiscuity, along with the defiance of authority, made such a merciless mark among too many adolescents that a more sober group of experts took to the media, advising a midcourse correction. These gurus said there must be at least *some* parental authority, *some* negative consequences for inappropriate (still avoiding the word "immoral") behavior of kids. These consequences should not be physical, of course — nothing violent, only therapeutic. The trouble was, this course "correction" was too little, too late, and so mild that it was ineffective. The gurus congratulated themselves on improving parenting — at the same time being unable to reverse in any significant way the negative consequences they had not foreseen. In the process, hundreds of years of wisdom were thrown out in the belief that the lives of our children would be better.

> **DISPATCH F**
> Sixteen-year-old Todd has put a padlock on his bedroom door so that his parents may not enter without his permission. Mom and Dad are afraid that they will only make matters worse if they do not comply with his wishes.

But the lives of our children were *not* better. They were becoming slowly more angry, lonely, and frustrated. The lives of the vast majority of America's kids were *not* so out of control (just about 5 percent are!) as to merit or require ungovernable status or recourse to juvenile courts or mental health practitioners, but you could see the anger and defiance in their eyes and in their clothes. You could hear it in their music and in their language. Life was failing too many American kids — not at the end, not at the middle, but at the very beginning.

As elements of the culture of childrearing in America became thoroughly anti-authoritarian, they slowly became more toxic. Parents did not want their children to be angry at them. Lying, cheating, or stealing became more open, not a matter to hide or be ashamed of. Ours became more of a self-centered culture, a culture of "I deserve it" and "I come first." This was well-described by Daniel Yankelovich, a famous analyst of social trends and the founder of a well-known public opinion polling company, in his book *New Rules: Searching for Self-Fulfillment in a World Turned Upside Down*. In this book, he shows how we have moved from an ethic of self-denial to an ethic of self-fulfillment. We have become a culture that teaches people to feel good about saying, "I will help others only to the degree that it helps me."

Eventually, parents had to face the fact that their adolescent children were not behaving well and were impacted by the environmental conditioning of an adolescent culture of drugs, alcohol, oppositional defiance, and much more. Parents were losing power. And, despite being told not to feel guilty about that, more often than not they *did* feel guilty about their failure to parent their children in a more healthy fashion.

In 1983, a Swiss psychoanalyst, Alice Miller, came to the aid of these parents. Her book *For Your Own Good: Hidden Cruelty in Child Rearing and the Roots of Violence* (1983) arrived on the shores of America with an ominous message: If you as a parent are unsuccessful in raising your children, the reason is simple. You yourselves have been victims, "unwitting slaves to the dark secrets of your own childhood."

Now, the rhetoric of almost universal victimhood entered American culture. It was okay to forget guilt because you, too, were a victim. Incredible as it seems, the author used Hitler as an example of a person who was a victim of his own childhood rather than the immoral monster that we all knew him to be. Her conclusion? "Don't feel guilty.

Nothing is ever gained by assigning guilt." And, by logical extension — don't put a guilt trip on your children.

> **DISPATCH G**
> Josh's behavior has made his mom, dad, and his two brothers and sister totally miserable — so miserable that Mom and Dad have rented him an apartment, provided him a car and are gladly telling others their sixteen-year-old son is happy in his independent living arrangement.

The implication was clear. It wasn't your fault or mine that we failed as parents. The culture had obviously not been kind enough to us when we were children and therefore, we ourselves were actually the victims. A gigantic new cultural rationalization soon afflicted the nation. When we did something wrong, we could always say it was not our fault because we were victims. We were told to just consult our "inner-child of the past" and try to recapture our own innocence before imposing anything on others.

This thinking had a profound impact on the educators and the other elite in America. It made them feel better for awhile — and more accepting of the fact that their children were, in their own words, "disaster areas."

In her next book, *The Drama of the Gifted Child* (1984), Alice Miller then said parents were committing a crime if they tried to inculcate traditional Christian values in their children. No, indeed; parents needed to let children decide for themselves. Reading this, the secularists had a heyday, and before long, they applied a new notion of freedom even to adolescents: *unlimited self-determination.* The idea was to give unlimited freedom and choice to kids — even though adults knew they were too immature to handle it, due to underdevelopment of the adolescent brain and the lower level of education they'd had in their lives thus far. Those common-sense rationales didn't apply: adolescents deserved that freedom anyway. And before long, the idea of unlimited self-determination took root in some of our courts as it grew popular among the elite.

Now, underdeveloped, unsophisticated adolescents leave lots to be desired in the area of decision making. Our experience at Boys Town with kids who bought into unlimited self-determination was that their lives were miserable, not happy. They didn't know how to get their needs met in pro-social ways. Many of the kids who came to us did not think they would live beyond eighteen because their unlimited self-determination resulted in addiction, abuse, violence, and other maladies that sap the ability of humans to flourish.

In a recent book, *The Death of the Grown-up* (2007), *Washington Times* syndicated columnist Diana West marshals together important research and story after story showing that adolescence is now prolonged in so many, many cases until age 30 or 31. Some call this a new stage of human development, namely emerging adulthood. She suggests these young adults are, in reality, perpetual adolescents. Perhaps she has a point, which we will look a little later.

In my early days as Executive Director of Boys Town in the 1980s, we developed some very traditional, authoritative parenting training that we called "Common Sense Parenting." It combined firm discipline with warmth and love. The U.S. Air Force Family Service Office compared our Common Sense Parenting with some other more permissive parenting strategies from other providers; their conclusion? The more permissive strategies and ours both made parents almost equally happy. What then was the difference? The more permissive strategies changed the attitudes of *parents* from feeling guilty to not feeling guilty. Ours changed the behavior of *children* from negative to positive behavior. Which do you think is more effective for a healthy society?

Almost anyone can see that moms and dads who buy into permissive parenting are being played as patsies. They are used and controlled by their children. At Boys Town, our hearts always go out to parents who have learned their permissive parenting skills from their children, their neighbors, their relatives, their schools, their community, and their environment. It is a contagious virus that infects many and makes many lives miserable.

We learn at Boys Town that the first step back to health for moms and dads is to realize that all is not lost — they don't have to be miserable, and they don't have to give up inculcating values and character in their children. They have to realize that they can instill in the hearts of their children a sense of responsibility and confidence, that there is a healthy way to teach skills and build relationships in a postmodern age. We can show them how to throw away the bad advice and how to learn new skills so that when their children lie, cheat, or steal, there is a little voice inside each boy or girl telling them they are going down the wrong road. The internal monitor can be prodded to activation by moms, dads, grandmas, and grandpas with a head and a heart: authoritative (not authoritarian) parents who are warm and nurturing, while imposing firm limits, demands, and controls.

This first dispatch is about how we got to where we are now. And where are we? At a hospital Intensive Care Unit where family and family authority are in stable, but critical condition. But the patient can be restored to health and hope. A wholesome family is possible, without relying on either authoritarian or permissive parenting methods. Skills can be learned. Relationships can be built up and strengthened. Parents can renew their courage and develop good parenting techniques. By word and example, children can be shown that if they want to be happy, they need to practice virtue. And, in the end, the fabric of the family can be restored.

We will see how in the next chapter.

# Chapter Two

# What Kind of Parenting Works Best

———◆———

*U need 2 no that adolescence iznt all storm n stress . . . mind u the generation gap iz now a myth. identity crises r propaganda . . . u uz disiplin w/warmth 4 best rezults.*

You need to know that adolescence isn't all storm and stress . . . mind you, the generation gap is now a myth . . . identity crises are propaganda . . . you use discipline with warmth for best results.

In this chapter, our "dispatch from the front" give you the inside scoop on what kind of parenting works best, based on lots of research, personal observation, and good practice. But let's begin by taking a critical look at a so-called truth we hear over and over again as our children enter adolescence — prepare for open warfare!

We are told that our children are going to break with us, to develop emotional independence, and we need to lighten up and go with the flow. We need to acknowledge the generation gap and learn to live with it. Similarly, as your children grow into adolescence, many of you will hear that they will have to experience a massive identity crisis, involving great conflict with parents, as they try to discover who they really are and break through the façade of what you have trained them to be. And for the past forty years, there has been a very loud, persistent media message to moms and dads and other authority figures such as teachers, coaches, ministers, and priests, that we need to lighten up on authority. We need to realize that manners and morals have changed, and you must let your children act accordingly — but, of course, at the same time you need to keep them safe (if you can).

All of this is wrong. It is all inaccurate. It is bad advice. (Except for the part about keeping your children safe!)

The great chasm that exists is between certain persistent messages of the permissive popular culture today — with accompanying hands-off messages to parents — and what the best research shows is really happening, what is good for our children, and what really works.

So let us start off with Laurence Steinberg, President of the Society for Research on Adolescence, who, at a 2001 convention, told the assembled researchers:

> There are some questions that have been so conclusively answered that it seems reasonable to suggest that no further research is needed on them and that efforts would be more fruitfully directed toward other issues.

The first question that the authorities say needs no more research is what kind of parenting works best. Yet Steinberg says that even though we know what is the best way to parent, "There has remained a dramatic disjunction between what is being said in academic circles and what is being sold to parents through the popular media."

Let us look at three examples he uses.

---

### DISPATCH A

High school graduation is Sunday. But let me tell you, I came here to commit suicide. My life was going nowhere. I had been in about 11, 12, or 13 placements so I wanted to run away to Boys Town and there end my life. My Family-Teachers let me share my horrible feelings about myself with them and so did my classmates Joey and Margareta, who are sitting here. We all talked about this often. They talked me out of suicide and repeatedly showed me life was worthwhile. I felt good expressing myself and felt even better to realize I owe them my very life itself.

— Georgia

Anna Freud, continuing the psychoanalytic approach of her father, announced repeatedly and solemnly that it was important as children move into adolescence to break with their parents, develop the independence of emotional distance, and move out of the childhood dependence on their moms and dads. Of course, children need to grow up to become adults. But does this mean that we can anticipate *open warfare* between the generations? Many parents are taught to expect that their children will no longer listen to them, hunger for emotional support or emotional strength, or have good relationships with grandparents. Research, however, shows this expectation isn't true.

Steinberg also uses the example of Erik Erikson, who popularized the idea in the '60s that adolescence necessarily entails a *massive identity crisis* involving a great deal of nasty, bitter conflict with mom and dad as their teenage sons and daughters try to discover who they really are by breaking through the façade of who they have been trained to be by their family. The parent-teen relationship is assumed to be open revolt or rebellion — or, in milder cases, guerilla warfare. But the key idea was the same: if you don't have an identity crisis, something must be wrong with you! (What a powerful impetus for trying drugs!)

In the 1960s, I remember seeing kids walking around literally saying, "I don't know who I am." It sounds bizarre, but it happened. Thank goodness, the craze for an identity crisis has somewhat passed with time; unfortunately, many people are still being told to expect some variety of it in their children.

**DISPATCH B**

When I came, I was going to prove to everyone how tough I was. I had lived on the streets, lived with a Crip and nobody messed with me. I had come out of a home with a crazoid mom. What I was trying to prove to people was that I could be a street person. Well, I could, but I knew it was not me. Why? Because two of my housemates, together with my Family-Teachers, helped me express these feelings and realize I had to find myself and be myself. It's amazing because when I did this, I started to find happiness.

— Josie

In the past few decades, popular TV commentators, journalists, and even preachers have bought into this "*storm and stress model*" and advised parents to live and let live. In other words, parents should expect teenagers to rebel, and they should then allow whatever experimentation and autonomy the teens demand. The adolescent, these folks said, was moving from childhood dependence to independence, and independence is a good thing. The theme of teen independence caught on in advertising campaigns of fashion and grooming, and even educators became sold on it. What hadn't yet dawned on the media was that beyond independence is a much more desirable state of *interdependence.*

In the 1970s, something happened by the way of research that — from an academic view, if not a media view — put a nail in the coffin of the idea that serious adolescent rebellion had to be normal, that parents could expect it, and that they should accommodate it as necessary and even desirable. Study after study showed that 75 percent of teenagers reported good, pleasing, happy, pleasant relationships with their moms and dads. So who was going through the "storm and stress," anyway?

Don't misunderstand these statistics: some of these adolescents may have been happy because they were successful in manipulating their parents! And certainly, the studies didn't mean that everyone was happy all the time. Of course, there were rocky times; there always are. There are always new challenges in the teen years, and they are often painful and hurtful. What it does mean is that if an identity crisis, or individuation, or whatever you called it, was happening (and something was happening), it wasn't having a tsunami-like effect on the relationship between adolescents and parents. In fact, further research into the unhappy 25 percent showed they had troubles long before adolescence, and the kids brought that baggage into their teen years.

If the idea of a "storm and stress" adolescence is now obsolete, the same is true of the idea so firmly entrenched in the American psyche of "*the generation gap.*" There *was* a generation gap, but for only a short time. Remember the

> **DISPATCH C**
>
> I was adopted at age six and pushed around from place to place. I went through the Treatment Group Home and Community One and finally found myself because my Family-Teachers helped me in every way possible. They disciplined me. They loved me. They listened to me a lot. They made me feel worthwhile, that I was not nothing. All in my home are the real reasons I got better.
>
> — Joey

hippies with their mantra of "no college, no conventional job, no middle-class house or lifestyle"? Compare that today with the adolescents who are interested in college and a middle-class lifestyle with an important, high-paying job. Our children today look nothing like the hippies. They don't act like the hippies. They don't believe what the hippies believed. They are far more middle-class by almost every measure, as materialistic and consumer-oriented as their moms and dads.

Another area where the media would have us believe that teenagers are miles and miles apart from their parents is religion. Certainly, some U.S. teens are alienated and rebellious when it comes to religious involvement. In some sections of the country — for example, the Northeast — going to church on Sunday is far, far less prominent among adolescents than adults. But more teens are like their parents in the area of religion than is commonly portrayed in the media. The National Study of Youth and Religion, in research conducted from July 2002 to March 2003, concurs:

> Contrary to many popular assumptions and stereotypes, the character of teenage religiosity in the United States is extraordinarily conventional. The vast majority of U.S. teens are not alienated or rebellious when it comes to religious involvement. Most are quite content to follow in their parents' footsteps.

Why, then, do some psychologists still buy into these outdated models? The answer might be what is called the therapist's illusion. If a therapist only sees adolescents with severe disorders, it's not unusual for them to believe that the vast majority of kids are just like those they see regularly. This is an occupational hazard of therapists. (It is also an occupational hazard of those who work at a residential place like Boys Town, who are tempted to believe that all kids are just like these.)

So, as we shall see, it is very bad advice to say that parents should globally allow their teens to indulge in foul language, live in filthy rooms, and/or use drugs, sex, and alcohol. Yes, there is conflict between parents and teens; there's also conflict between workers and bosses, moms and dads, little children and parents. Conflict is part of being human, not some special domain of teenagers, and we have to stop catastrophizing adolescence!

This period of raising a child doesn't have to be all-out war. But let's be honest. Adolescence can be stressful. What research now suggests is that adolescents today have specific challenges: namely, different senses of right and wrong (morality), common courtesy, and acceptable civilized behavior. Now, these things do cause stress for moms and dads as kids try to get parents to accept their ideas. This is where moms and dads have to decide who's in charge and which of these should be made major battles and which just minor skirmishes.

Let us look at each of these three:

- *A different sense of right or wrong.* This is principally concerned with sexual behavior, drugs, and alcohol. The culture and the media are stacked against parents in regard to right and wrong. Yes, it will be a struggle, but it is one that you can win with warmth, firmness, and skill.

- *A different sense of common courtesy.* This ranges all the way from rudeness, poor hygiene, and snotty language to such simple things as lack of saying "please" and "thank you." Again, this is an area where parents can have a major influence.

- *A different sense of acceptable civilized behavior.* This includes living in filthy rooms, wearing baggy and sagging clothing, sporting visible tattoos, cutting, and oppositional/defiant behavior in matters large and small. Adolescents try to wear their parents down in this regard, and parents must be prepared for this.

None of these issues has to become nuclear war; they can all remain minor skirmishes. The good news is that the insistence that children must honor their father and their mother — an insistence that is bolstered by prayer, warmth, and self-assurance — will win out in the end. Remember how you responded to your children when they were very small and "nattering" you? Similar solutions are available for adolescent "nattering," solutions we'll discuss a little later.

So what kind of parenting actually works? It's not *permissive parenting*. It's not *authoritarian parenting*. It's something that both researchers and Boys Town practitioners call *authoritative parenting*.

Clinical and developmental psychologist Diana Baumrind, best known for her research on parenting styles, describes the popular permissive ideological parenting in the following way:

> The permissive parent attempts: to behave in a nonpunitive, acceptant, and affirmative manner toward the child's impulses, desires, and actions. She consults with him about policy decisions and gives explanations for family rules. She makes few demands for household responsibility and orderly

> behavior. She presents herself to the child as a resource for him to use as he wishes, not as an active agent responsible for shaping or altering his ongoing or future behavior. She allows the child to regulate his own activities as much as possible, avoids the exercise of control, and does not encourage him to obey externally-defined standards. She attempts to use reason but not overt power to accomplish her ends.[1, 2]

It should surprise no one at all to find the research confirms that permissive parenting rates at the bottom on almost every scale or measure. Very few parents, Baumrind found, actually fit the strict criteria for this, but many agonize over their teenagers bombarding them with narrating messages of "This isn't fair" and "You have to trust me to make my own decisions."

The second type of parenting — *authoritarian* — is attractive to some parents. In this model, the parents are the boss, period. One reason some parents find it appealing is that these children score quite well on avoidance of drugs and alcohol. They do well in avoiding other deviant behaviors. They score reasonably well on

---

[1] First paper where prototypes are published: Baumrind, D. (1966),"Effects of Authoritative Parental Control on Child Behavior." *Child Development,* 37(4), 887-907. Second, and most often cited, paper with extensive discussion of parenting styles: Baumrind, D. (1967),"Child care practices anteceding three patterns of preschool behavior." *Genetic Psychology Monographs,* 75(1), 43-88.

[2] Ibid.

> **DISPATCH D**
>
> When I came I had been very badly sexually abused. I didn't care about anything. I felt worthless. My body wasn't even mine. It belonged to those who abused me. I wanted to quit life. I wanted to give up. My friends, Mary and Kashina, and my Family-Teachers got me through day after day after day. They kept listening to me. They kept talking to me. They kept being with me and they kept me here, and that is the only reason I made it.
>
> — Salena

conforming to their parents' standards. The families don't have constant warfare, but authoritarian parents overwhelm their children into obedience. The price paid for that obedience is often depression, loneliness, and alienation, along with anger and anxiety.

So what's the alternative? Baumrind describes it this way:

> An authoritative parent attempts: to direct the child's activities but in a rational issue-oriented manner. She encourages verbal

give and take, and shares with the child the reasoning behind her policy. She values both expressive and instrumental attributes, both autonomous self-will and disciplined conformity. Therefore, she *exerts firm control at points of parent-child divergence,* but does not hem the child in with restrictions. She recognizes her own special rights as an adult, but also the child's individual interests and special ways. The authoritative parent affirms the child's present qualities, but also sets standards for future conduct. *She uses reason as well as power to achieve her objectives.* She does not base her decisions on group consensus or the individual child's desires; but also, does not regard herself as infallible or divinely inspired (emphasis added).

Baumrind's original studies gained the attention of other researchers who, over decades, have reaffirmed and refined again and again that this is the way to go for parents.

You may agree that authoritative parenting is the best for younger children. But what about teenagers? Steinberg again:

Perhaps the most important conclusion to emerge from our work is that adolescents raised in authoritative homes continue to show the same advantages in psycho-social development and mental health over their non-authoritatively raised peers

> that were apparent in studies of younger
> children. Adolescents from authoritative
> homes achieve more in school, report less
> depression and anxiety, score higher on
> measures of self-reliance and self-esteem,
> are less likely to engage in any social behavior
> including delinquency and drug use.

So let's take a closer look at these three parenting approaches.

The **permissive approach** involves inconsistency with no clear limits, makes feeble demands, and has no firm controls. Most permissive parents fall into one of the two categories. The first is the *permissive neglectful approach*. This consists of off-again and on-again warmth, with laxity in conscience formation of the children. The children are out of control because the caretakers do not have the skill set or the desire needed to be successful. Oftentimes moms and dads will say, "This is all we can do." They know no other way; they just don't want their children angry with them. This is the most common variety of family dysfunctionality we see with children who come to Boys Town.

The second is the *permissive indulgent approach*, involving a smaller group of parents who believe that control and command are counterproductive. A good example of this approach comes from the mother of a sixteen-year-old in Florida. When asked how her son became so oppositional and defiant, his mother answered:

> My husband and I did everything the child
> psychologists told us to do. We did not
> discipline our son; we encouraged him. When
> he came in late, we provided him with a kind
> of counseling approach. When he received
> F's, we surrounded him with more care and
> concern. We did everything the counseling
> people told us to do, and this is the result.

The **authoritarian approach** puts strict limits and controls without much perceived warmth. This is often seen in families where parents don't pay sufficient attention to their children's behavior until they are out of control, and then the parents pounce on them with physical and emotional punishment.

Another example is seen in some military families. The father takes his chain-of-command home after work, treating his children as lowly recruits. The result is, more often than not, severe dysfunctionality in the lives of children such as depression, anxiety, alienation, and anger. When there is conformity, rebellion is never far away.

The third approach is **authoritative parenting** — using warmth, caring, and sharing, combined with strict limits and controls. Both the limits and controls and warmth and caring have to be age appropriate. This is the approach we have used successfully for decades here at Boys Town. We introduced it in the late 1970s, when we joined forces with Kansas University's Achievement Place, the NIMH (National Institutes of Mental Health), and the U.S. Dept.

> **DISPATCH E**
> When I came here, I wanted to throw away my life and, Katie, you befriended me. You told me I could not do that because you cared about me and my Family-Teachers cared about me and they listened and they let me make choices which were hard to make. You were the only ones I knew of who cared, so you saved my life. Thank you.
>
> — Margareta

of Justice in developing behavior-shaping techniques that later became known as the Boys Town Model.

At first, our approach was more authoritarian than authoritative, with more clinical behaviorism than family warmth. But nothing starts out with a perfect mixture, and our model gradually gained more balance over forty years. During my twenty-year administration, we made a significant effort to bring in much more warmth, and the results were quite encouraging and satisfying. We say today that the head (discipline) without the heart (warmth) is pure manipulation. The heart (warmth) without the head (discipline) is pure sentimentality.

Our model begins with behavior on the outside and works toward character development, conscience formation, and moral uprightness on the inside. It needs a family setting and begins with teaching family skills to our children and building relationships. These family skills at first sound so simple: following instructions, taking "no" for an answer, accepting negative feedback, and many others. They are the bedrock of civilization, the roots of happiness and even joy. The key here is the proper relationship between a high amount of warmth and very low tolerances for behaviors. If you combine large amounts of warmth with very low tolerances and use approximations in a behavioral setting, you usually get good results.

Of course, we need to tweak the model regularly as we learn more and more and as the culture of our children and families changes. In addition to warmth and low tolerances, what we are working on at the present time is *psychological autonomy*. This refers to the way adolescents subjectively experience their parents as allowing them to express their feelings, granting those feelings importance, and promoting give-and-take, as well as feelings of self-confidence and self-competence. If the family culture is too psychologically controlling (not allowing expression of emotional needs or autonomy), this will hurt an adolescent's self-image. Psychological autonomy can, in many cases, shield a youth from too much anxiety, depression, and loneliness. Recent studies indicate the importance of psychological autonomy for healthy emotional development, bringing about a better sense of control over one's life (including impulse control) and pride in one's efforts. A better sense of control over one's life is an enormous benefit in a culture striving for just the opposite — namely, environmental conditioning.

The question we are asking at Boys Town is whether psychological autonomy will help with behavioral self-control when Boys Town's behavioral control is no longer present. In other words, if we combine emotional autonomy with close ties to a parental figure — someone who loves

---

### DISPATCH F

My mom is an alcoholic. She had a new boyfriend every day, someone to buy booze for her. It hurt me as a little girl, hurt me more than I can say. My Family-Teachers were the first parents I ever had. They listened to me and cared about me. They wouldn't let me get away with things and they let me try out new things. They did everything to bring me the love and affection and structure I never had.
— Chrystal

---

you and holds you accountable — will better behavior continue even when the teen is on his or her own? We think so. We hope so. We believe so.

So, knowing that authoritative parenting works best with today's youth, let us start practicing this style with grace, faith, and confidence. Especially when it comes to a new challenge on the parenting frontlines — Perpetual Adolescence.

# Chapter Three

# Perpetual Adolescence

*U need 2 no adolesens is not ovr @ hs graduation
. . . it lasts u 2 age 30 . . . unless u take action now . . .
help ur teen gro up.*

You need to know adolescence is not over at high
school graduation . . . it lasts you to age 30 . . . unless
you take action now . . . help your teen grow up.

This third "dispatch from the front" reveals something
quite astonishing: that when kids graduate from high
school, our culture allows them not to be "adults" yet;
they don't grow up until their early 30s. Many parents still
assume that graduation from high school is what it used
to be, namely, a milestone in moving from adolescence to
adulthood — but it's not so anymore. If you doubt this,
ask yourself if you've noticed many young men and women
in their 20s spending five, six, or seven years in college (or
more than one!), moving from job to job, or perhaps living
at home and not settling down. Have you noticed how
many young men and women drop out of college, work
$8-an-hour jobs, and move frequently? It is a huge shift
in the way young Americans, ages 18 to 30-plus, perceive
themselves. Once you understand this shift, you can be
equipped to deal successfully with this very different
younger generation.

In her 2007 book, Diana West calls this *The Death of the Grown-up*. She points out that, in 2002, the National Academy of Sciences formally recognized that adolescence extends from puberty at least to age 30. In addition, in 2003, the MacArthur Foundation presided over a research project that pegged age 34 as the time when most young Americans enter into adulthood. They come out of a group of people aged 18 to 30 who have now been labeled "emerging adults" or "extended adolescents." This is seen as a new stage in life between adolescence and full-blown adulthood. And — just in case you might be wondering — it's not an occasion for celebration! As West quotes Eric Hoffer:

> If a society is to preserve its stability and a degree of continuity, it must know how to keep its adolescents from imposing their tastes, attitudes, values, and fantasies on the everyday world. This has serious implications for how we relate to these perpetual adolescents.

I once was roundly chastised when, in a speech about this matter, I criticized U2's Bono for saying at the Grammy Awards that he planned to keep "F—ing up the mainstream." Despite all the good he does (and he does tremendous good), that attitude is simply, and quite unintentionally, giving young people permission not to grow up.

Let me give you an example of this prolonged adolescence. Jeremy, 29, joined the Air Force doing basic training at Lackland Air Force Base in San Antonio and advanced training in computers in Mississippi. After his turn of duty was over, he moved back to his hometown and married his girlfriend. He is good at programming, understands systems, and loves video games. In fact, he camped out from midnight on at Best Buy to be one of the first to purchase Halo III the next morning. He spends most of his weekends (endless hours) playing video games, especially Grand Theft Auto IV. Like Peter Pan, he has never grown up and feels no need to do so. But his wife is divorcing this perpetual adolescent. She wants an adult for a husband — a friend, not a webmaster and gamer for their four-year-old son. And Jeremy cannot understand why.

I see examples of this type of delayed adulthood every day in working with graduates of Boys Town. They are not exceptions; in this regard, they fit into the mainstream. Researchers say this time of extended adolescence is characterized by five phenomena embedded in our culture:

## 1) Emerging adults are convinced that "you can be whatever you want to be."

This common notion — that success waits just around the corner — pervades senior classes graduating from high schools across the country; many of them have found it hard to cope with real life when it turns out to be false. They never anticipated what would face them in the school of life when they left the life of high school. And this even was before our recent economic collapse.

Joe wants to be a surgeon, but cannot pass neuroanatomy. Alyssa wants to be an oceanographer, but there are no jobs available. Lilly chose law as a profession but cannot score well on the LSAT. College professors are not prone to inspire perseverance in so many students with inappropriate aspirations, but this doesn't stop Joe, Alyssa, or Lilly from drifting for five to ten years before they "grow up." A friend of mine teaching freshman biology at an elite university often says, "I have a class of 300 freshmen in general biology every semester. Almost all of them want to be physicians. My job is to convince 90 percent of them to seek other careers."

## 2) Emerging adults are convinced that self-esteem is all important.

As Charles Sykes says in *50 Rules Kids Won't Learn in School*, "Your high school may have done away with winners and losers. Life hasn't." In primary and secondary American education, students are regularly applauded for everything they do. But upon graduation, it's hard to maintain your self-esteem when that applause is no longer there. It's hard to maintain self-esteem when you come in late for work and get fired. (Why don't they understand that I overslept?) It's hard to maintain self-esteem when your every idea is no longer lauded. (Don't they understand how good my ideas are?) It's hard to maintain self-esteem when your company outsources your job and you are surplused.

One of the characteristics of this extended-adolescent culture is the clash between the sobering realities of the workaday world and self-esteem. It may take years to realize your self-esteem was built on quicksand.

<hr>

**DISPATCH A**

Jeanine graduated in the mediocre middle of her high school class and told her family she needed to rest for a few months before going to college. She spent the summer chilling. She had not taken the ACT or SAT seriously and was not eligible for most four-year colleges, so she entered a community college. Before the end of the first quarter she stopped going to class, but still lived in the dorms and had a full meal plan which she took advantage of. She received a $1,800 Pell Grant, which was free money, and two Stafford loans that would have to be repaid. She said that the school officials would not find out for some time that she was not in class. So she lived in the dorms until Thanksgiving and then departed college life to go back home.

<hr>

3) **Emerging adults are sure it's unnecessary to conform to rules.**

"Kids emerge from adolescence with a view that conformity to rules is stupid," says Jean Twenge in *Generation Me*. Emerging adults can, in some cases, be shielded from violation of rules by their parents; eventually, however, the rubber hits the road.

You fail to appear in court for a traffic violation, a warrant goes out for your arrest, and you're picked up and spend time in jail. A youthful DUI will appear on your record for years and years. What employer wants to hire you with that on your record?

---

### DISPATCH B

In his senior year of high school, Johnny's mom and dad could not bring themselves to tell him that the appropriate choices for him (under the circumstances of too many sports and too little learning) after graduation were either working at a $10-an-hour job, military service, or Job Corps. He was not ready for college. He had wonderful, kind, permissive parents who said yes when he wanted to go to college. He enrolled, did not go much to classes and left his college dorm and the university at Christmas, when he was welcomed home and took a full-time job at Burger King at $7.00 an hour. Johnny is a perpetual adolescent.

Or perhaps something happens that's not quite so serious, but still eye-opening: you thought your debit card would stop your spending when the balance hit zero, but with the insurance provision it allows you to borrow $500 — and now, you're in arrears; or your cell phone is shut off when your unpaid bill reaches $3,400.

Learning that you have to conform can be very difficult for some emerging adults.

## 4) Emerging adults are strongly convinced there is easy access to sexual fulfillment.

There is easy access to sexual *activity*. Sexual *fulfillment*, however, is another thing altogether. Young women are most vulnerable in this regard. They move in with one fellow for a few months, and then another, and another, and another. Their heart is broken repeatedly, as failed romances, more often than not, are quickly followed by romances on the rebound. This is more than harmful . . . just as HPV (human papillomavirus) is very common and more than harmful.

An interesting irony arises from this perpetual adolescence: on one hand, young men and women can believe there are no moral restraints on sexual activity (or lying or cheating) — yet on the other hand, they'll substitute strictness in surprisingly insignificant areas, almost as if to show they stand for something. For instance, the vast majority of these young people believe that you should never ever use a product that has an expired shelf life, you should always answer your text messages right away, you should never eat without washing your hands, and you should never let your partner's sexual needs go unmet.

The other day I was with a 24-year-old girl at a gas station when a middle-aged lady at the next pump spilled a bit of gasoline. The girl said to me, "We need to do something about that. It's very wrong to leave that gas on the ground." When I told her it was only a small puddle, and to leave it alone, she was incensed . . . and yet, she was on pot. You could see it in her eyes. She didn't notice the glaring contrast between great concern about a little spilled gas and her lack of concern about something far worse: pot smoking.

## 5) Emerging adults tend to believe that life is all about consumption and gratification.

In this time of economic collapse, the belief that life is all about consumption clashes with the grim reality of wanting more and having less. Frequent job loss leads to ill-considered jobs, such as selling expensive vacuum cleaners door-to-door, or outbound telemarketing jobs that pay only commission, when you have no salesmanship skills. Many emerging adults have stiffed at least one cell phone company, failing to pay their bills and easily securing another cell phone from another company. At least nobody goes hungry: there's plenty of Ramen noodles and frozen pizza around. But the culture of thrift has vanished, replaced by the lottery culture.

My own experience at Boys Town is that kids who come out of foster care, the juvenile justice system, and the mental health system are especially at risk to suffer from the phenomena described here. They are much more likely to suffer anxiety and depression from the disconnect between their cherished beliefs and the cold reality of the world in which they live. They are much more likely to be exceptionally stressed by this disconnect, yet highly skilled in never going hungry.

---

### DISPATCH C

After graduation, Mariah went to the University of Minnesota. She liked school, changed her major three times, and is now in her sixth and final year in college. She likes this life a lot with her family paying for tuition, room, and board. She is planning to go to graduate school and is living with her boyfriend, the third boyfriend she has lived with in six years of college. No one is requiring her to move beyond this adolescent lifestyle. No one is requiring her to grow up.

---

Professor Christian Smith of Notre Dame points out how important it is to recognize this new stage of life and come to grips with it. He also points to some of the common feeling-states research that shows the following characteristics of these emerging adults ages 18 to 32:

loneliness, depression, apprehension, and abundance of sarcasm. These feeling states go hand in hand with a long series of live-in boyfriends/girlfriends, spending sprees, pot smoking, drug use, and leaving town with no forwarding address to avoid court appearances for shoplifting, speeding, and drug charges. Even if the emerging adult uses only one or two, not all, of these strategies, these coping mechanisms are commonplace — and self-destructive.

Let me share with you *four secret ways* you can help the young people in your life grow up and be successful in family and economic life. Use them gently, compassionately, and with much warmth. Here goes:

## 1) Realize that the promise you were given to believe in high school — namely, that you can be whatever you want to be — is bunk.

As Jason Enke says it, in his book *100 Things You Did Not Learn in School,* young people are wise to look realistically at their skills and abilities. Dream *big* dreams, but *big realistic* dreams. If you are academically deficient in science and math, don't plan to go into the medical or nursing field unless you plan some remedial work in the future. Otherwise, it's unrealistic. If you are emotionally immature, do not even bother starting college. You'll just be wasting money and spinning your wheels. You can tell whether you are emotionally immature by going to someone such as your mother or father or an honest, wise teacher, and ask them. They'll tell you.

### DISPATCH D

Dakota joined the Army after high school, did well in basic training and, graduating shortly before Christmas, went home on leave. He looked forward after leave to going to AIT (Advanced Infantry Training) in Maryland and learning how to be a Humvee mechanic. That seemed appealing. But during Christmas leave, he fell into his old high school habit of smoking marijuana and, as he says in his own words, "I just never got around to reporting for duty at AIT." So now he is AWOL (Absent without Leave). He put away his uniform, lives with two of his high school buddies, and has a job flipping burgers at McDonald's. After six months of AWOL, a soldier automatically becomes a deserter, which is a felony. The other day he was stopped by the State Highway Patrol for speeding. They looked up his record and immediately handcuffed him and took him to jail. Ten days later, two Military Police returned him to Fort Riley, Kansas, where he was dishonorably discharged. He is currently living with his mother.

In other words, develop a realistic plan to achieve realistic dreams, a plan that has some chance of success.

If you are financially unable to pay for college, or emotionally immature, or both . . . consider a hitch in the armed forces. Just remember: the Army is not a treatment facility. It has a mission; you have a soldier's job to do. *BDUs* (Battle Dress Uniforms) are not Halloween costumes. If you can't do the mission, don't join.

But if you understand and are prepared to do the hitch right, you'll get three benefits from going into the military.

First, you serve your country. People will always be proud of you for that . . . very proud of you. No matter what they think of wars in Afghanistan or anywhere else, many people will be proud of you because you're willing to serve.

Second, you can learn a trade or a skill in the military that will help later on in life, either as preparation for college or continued work in the field. For example, if you go into computers or intelligence, security or culinary arts, supply or logistics, it will hold you in good stead in the future.

Finally, you will gain emotional maturity, so that when you are honorably discharged, you can start life honorably — not as a perpetual adolescent.

2) **Push the self-esteem movement out of your mind and out of your life. That's not the end of your dreams; it's the end of empty dreams.**

If you want to feel good about yourself, accomplish something. Do it day after day after day. Self-esteem follows good behavior; it doesn't precede it. In the words of Charles Sykes, "You are not a victim. So stop whining."

It is important that we adults who surround these young people let them know with great love and warmth that our expectation is that they will begin acting like adults and not like perpetual high school students.

## 3) Understand the necessity of following the rules. Yes, *all* the rules.

Life goes better that way. It reduces troubles and avoids discouragement in your life. If you pay your rent, your landlord will not evict you. If you get a traffic ticket, follow the rules, and appear in court for whatever you were charged with, no warrant will be issued for your arrest and you will not spend a night in jail. Don't overdraw your bank account; otherwise, the bank will charge you $10 a day. Don't run away from your debts because they will stay on your record. Equifax has a long, long memory.

Accept that sleeping around is not a remedy for loneliness and, surely, not a good preparation for marital happiness. Neither are drugs or alcohol. When I taught at the university level, we used to say of the incoming freshmen that we could tell the first week who was a real freshman and who was still in high school . . . by their behavior. Run around with successful peers and imitate them. If you associate with people who are on the road to success, then you will probably be on the road to success. In other words, if you want to be happy, practice virtue. As the old saying goes: If you lie down with dogs, you get up with fleas. It is ancient wisdom verified over the centuries and applicable to you today.

### DISPATCH E

Brian, 31, has been an alcoholic for 14 years. Alcoholism runs in his family, and that includes his dad, uncles, and grandfather. At 16, he did the common high school drinking rituals with his friends and says wistfully, "I remember the first time I got drunk. I liked it a lot." It didn't seem like much of a problem in high school because it was just weekend binge drinking. He was a so-so student. He said his family believed adolescence was a time for spreading his wings and trying new things. He often drank with his father. In college, Brian attended many parties and he knew in his heart of hearts he was drowning in a river of alcohol. He barely passed his courses, barely graduated, and since then has had one divorce, two marriages, three kids, four DUIs, and five jobs.

And moms and dads, with great love and warmth, help the young women in your family to realize that they are the biggest losers in the vast campaign to make them over-eroticized. Young men have always been predatory and are even more so in their extended adolescence. If this is a game, then girls play it for higher stakes and are more likely to lose.

## 4) Realize that life is not principally about consumption and gratification, but about preparing yourself for taking your role in adult society.

After graduation, don't "chill." Get a job right away. Not a $6.75 high school job, but one that pays at $10.50 or more an hour. It may not sound like much, but it's better than flipping fast-food burgers. In other words, start leaving adolescence behind, because the joys of the adult society are greater than you can possibly imagine — far greater than the joys of adolescence. They await you who grow up.

For instance, adult friendship is a blessing beyond words. It holds you in stead in good times and in bad. It is even better when your best friend is your wife or husband. There is nothing finer. It is the greatest joy. The second greatest joy will be your children. Adolescents may not recognize this because they see childhood and adolescence as a difficult time for themselves. Parents, however, see things differently.

- It's fun for parents to help little children share.

- It's fun to listen to the language children use when they play house in an affirming manner.

- It's fun to watch them be active playing games such as jump rope.

- It's fun to read them stories.

- It's fun to sit down at the table and share ice cream and cake and not just serve it.

- It's fun to hear your little ones ask questions like why they think rain comes down instead of going up and why the sun comes up in the east instead of the west.

- It's fun to share nature with them.

- It's fun to collect leaves.

- It's fun to plant a garden and weed it and till it and watch it grow together.

- It's fun to share with them what you like, such as baking cookies and making pies.

- It's fun to do Thanksgiving things and Christmas things and Lenten things and Easter things and Fourth of July things.

- It's fun to raise little children.

And, as your children grow into emerging puberty and adolescence, it's fun to practice authoritative parenting.

Of course, into everyone's life a little rain must fall, but all the great saints and all the great heroes have reminded themselves of four things that we should remind ourselves of each morning:

Life is sometimes hard.

But God is always good.

Praised be the name of the Lord.

PUSH. (Pray until something happens.)

How do you help your children leave adolescence behind? The short answer can be summed up in three mottoes: "Wake up, grow up, keep it up!"

## Wake Up!

What does this mean? Take Lucinda. At 17, she had her neck tattooed, without asking herself what she was going to look like when she was 50, 60, or 70. Her neck will be all wrinkled, the tattoo will be shriveled, and this will be a source of sadness, not gladness. She really has to wake up and, if possible, have it removed.

Saying "wake up" is the same as saying "sober up." Be realistic. The adult world has more positive, rewarding experiences than adolescents could possibly imagine, and they need to look forward to them. Of course, the academic world and the workaday world will never reward adolescent behavior, even less so in a slumping economy. They may tolerate it; they don't reward it because the academic world and the world of work look at immature adolescents not as rebels without a cause, but as pathetic. (Certain so-called universities are an exception. They will give As and Bs in exchange for high tuition. They give the appearance of learning, rather than the substance of learning . . . but that just makes waking up harder yet.)

To wake up means to see the goodness of so much of adult life.

## Grow Up!

There are joys of adulthood — namely, friendship, and later marriage and family — that an adolescent cannot experience. Most perpetual adolescents still believe in what is called the "radical freedom of absolute self-determination." The more they believe in and practice it, the less likely are they to be truly free and the more likely they are to become frustrated. They discover they're not "inventing" themselves (as they thought they would), but rather, that they're actually harming themselves, over and over again, and slipping into a morass of the banal.

One of the great joys of adulthood is a successful marriage and family. The experience of being husband and wife, father and mother, can be so rewarding that it needs to be embraced and cherished with gusto.

In addition, one of the best grownup experiences is to discover the joy of learning. I remember talking to Robbie, who came to us at the beginning of his junior year in high school barely able to read. He struggled with phonics and vocabulary. It would have been much easier for him not to grow up, but with lots of encouragement and warmth, he faced the challenge. At first he found reading to be no fun. It took great effort. But then one day, he picked up the sports page and was excited to read about his favorite NFL team, the Minnesota Vikings. For that one moment, reading became exciting — yes, exciting. He grew up that day because after that he not only discovered the joy of reading; he also began to discover the joy of learning about history, geography, and so many other things. The whole adult world had begun to open to him.

He went on to be successful in college, now has a good job, is married, and has children. He says what a blessing to have a wife as a mate in life, someone who is also a grownup whom he can really trust and who is his best friend. He said, above all, his children are the joy of his life. He is experiencing with them things he never had in his own life. And all these experiences would never have been available to him had he remained a perpetual adolescent.

## Keep It Up!

To keep up the momentum, you need food for this long journey in life. And there are three big items on the menu of a successful adult life.

The first one is our daily bread of joy and sadness. An adult learns how to bring warmth to the table of life, how to choose joy. It takes self-discipline and faith, hope and love. An adult can be a wellspring of goodness. Many adults learn much when sadness and tragedy are quartered in their house. An adult learns that joy is not the absence of sorrow. Joy is the sorrow that has been worked through.

### Dispatch F — The Positive!

Jessica had plenty to be angry about. Her family was dysfunctional with alcoholism, drugs, and unemployment. Her father was nowhere to be found. Her mother was codependent. Alcohol and drugs were everywhere. She had not much experience being loved and cared for. But when she left high school, she joined the U.S. Navy and discovered a band of sisters and brothers who cared for one another. She achieved mightily at the Naval Honor Guard Battalion in Washington, DC, as an honor guard at major events in Arlington Cemetery, the U.S. Capitol, and even the White House. She stood guard for the funeral of President Gerald Ford. She set aside anger, woke up, and started to find the sun was shining in her life. She realized that she was not just a victim. She could move beyond that.

It is Good Friday that leads to Easter Sunday. There is no other way.

The second item is the bread of life, the spiritual food for the journey. An adolescent can barely begin to imagine how powerful it is to be in touch with the Lord, to receive his grace and his strength. To eat the bread of life often is, over time, to experience real hope.

And the last item is to eat humble pie when necessary. That may sound like a terrible thing to do, but all of us adults who have eaten our share of humble pie know how good it is for us and how we need to thank the Lord for giving us the grace to do so. Without humility, gratitude is impossible.

CHAPTER FOUR

# Virtue and Self-Esteem

———— ⋘◉⋙ ————

*U need 2 no self esteem is ovr sold . . . much self esteem u find ineffective . . . a mezur of disiplin n virtue is better . . . don't bleev othrwyz.*

You need to know self-esteem is oversold . . . much self-esteem you find ineffective . . . a measure of discipline and virtue is better . . . don't believe otherwise.

The fourth "dispatch from the front" is about self-esteem, which pretty much everybody — including emerging adults — thinks is the key to young people's success. However, living on the front lines, dealing with the troubles and dysfunctionalities of America's children and families for two decades, you learn the real truth involved with "self-esteem," and that information is an eye-opener.

The arguments in favor of using self-esteem as a measurement and predictor of success are mostly based on what some call common sense. It would just make sense, some say, to think that we'll do better if we have a "can-do" attitude. It seems to make sense to assume that our children will perform better if their teachers praise them and spare the rod. But is that the case?

In 1986, California state government mandated and funded the idea that the self-esteem of all Californians should be raised. They were confident the result would be reductions in crime, drug addiction, unwanted pregnancies and welfare numbers. So they created the California Task Force to Promote Self-Esteem and Personal and Social Responsibility.

---

**DISPATCH A**

Anna, a senior, scored a 14 on her ACT test, doing very poorly in reading comprehension. (You should know that the NCAA requires a score of 17 for a young man to be eligible for NCAA Division I football.) It's obvious that Anna is a poor reader, but her response to her score is, "How can that be possible? I have always gotten good grades in reading comprehension."

---

Before rollout, the Task Force wisely thought they should do a little research because they were sure scholarly studies would show a close connection between lack of self-esteem and these social ills. Keep in mind that they were not neutral — they wanted very much to show a connection. The result? Studies showed almost *no* correlation between self-esteem and social ills. In other words, actual statistics showed that the social issues of crime, chemical addiction, unwanted pregnancies, and welfare dependency were not significantly impacted by raising self-esteem. And yet the idea of improving people's self-esteem as an all-purpose elixir has remained embedded in our culture.

Now before we go any further, it's true that solid research shows that people with high self-esteem are happier, more willing to undertake difficult tasks and re-energize themselves when times get tough. Some evidence suggests that those with high self-esteem may holistically leave behind projects that don't work, and medical evidence suggests that self-esteemers even have a lesser danger of heart disease. Those are the upsides.

But the *Harvard Mental Health Letter* (*HMHL*) points to other research studies that tell a very different story. Criminals, in general, do not suffer from low self-esteem; nor do drug dealers or pedophiles. And even among noncriminal populations, many people with high self-esteem are often perceived to be arrogant know-it-alls, overestimating their potential.

According to the *Harvard Mental Health Letter*, critics of the self-esteem movement say some of its advocates are suffering from a "clinician's illusion." What does that mean? It means that people go to therapists because they do not feel good about themselves. People who feel good about themselves and have high self-esteem (even if they are serial killers, narcissists, and rapists) don't usually go to a therapist. So, criminals with high self-esteem rarely see a therapist. Drug dealers are notoriously high self-esteemers who don't regularly avail themselves of therapeutic intervention. Pedophiles are often high self-esteemers.

People who behave immorally but have high self-esteem see no reason to go to a therapist, so they don't. But if a clinician mostly sees patients who combine low self-esteem and bad behavior, this may give him or her the false impression that people who behave badly have low self-esteem. The research shows, however, that the perceived link between self-esteem and bad behavior may all be an illusion.

The self-esteem movement is the flower child of Abraham Maslow, Erik Erikson, Carl Rogers, Eric Berne, and Thomas Harris, to name a few. These leaders did some fine things, but not in this arena. Discipline, punishment, and guilt, they said, are harmful. Do not engage in these practices. Be counselors and therapists instead. "If unconditional positive regard can help sick people," said Carl Rogers, "think what good it can do for well people."

The results of the movement have been surprisingly disappointing and thoroughly disheartening. California's efforts are one example. The self-esteem movement makes us lose our communitarian focus in exchange for an almost narcissistic self focus, which means that the self-esteem movement ends up hurting more than it helps. "Have I loved myself enough today?" is not a good place to start.

In a 1996 essay titled "The Self-Esteem Fraud," Ninah Shokraii (well known for *School Choice 2000), says:*

> For all of its current popularity, however, Self-Esteem threatens to deny children the tools they will need in order to experience true success in schools and as adults. Compelling research from around the world

> lends empirical proof to the traditional claim
> that achievement precedes self-esteem.
> There is, in fact, almost no link between
> low self-esteem and any number of social
> pathologies.

In the May 2003 issue of *Psychological Science in the Public Interest*, four well-known academics reviewed the existing literature on the benefits of self-esteem. They also found no significant link between high self-esteem and achievement in school, successful interpersonal relationships, or even healthy lifestyles.

And yet, the permissive parenting movement is still touting self-esteem.

Self-esteemers are like crabgrass in our cultural front yard. Once crabgrass gets started, it's very hard to get rid of. Too many citizens cling to permissive parenting and the elixir of self-esteem, despite frequently counter-intuitive results that are clear to see in countless schools across the country. As Dana Mack, senior fellow at the Center for Education Studies, points out, "Feeling good about reading doesn't make good readers." Nor does feeling good about writing make good writers; nor does feeling good about arithmetic make good mathematics students, or feeling good about your values make you a person of character, or feeling good about the way you treat your girlfriend mean you have a solid friendship.

The point is that performance precedes self-esteem. Anyone who has ever played basketball knows that you start by learning how to pass, dribble, and run and shoot.

You are quite awkward at first and don't feel good about yourself, but the more you work at it, the better you become, and the better you feel about yourself as a basketball player.

By contrast, one of my coworkers, George, related that when his sixth-grade son was cleaning out his room, he brought out a box of 15 to 20 trophies and asked if it was okay to throw them away. They were trophies he received for merely participating in various sports events. They clearly didn't mean anything to him.

Low self-control and high self-esteem are a recipe for disaster. Instead of simply raising children with high self-esteem, it is much more important to inculcate the values of hard work and virtue in our children. You acquire the virtue of honesty by disciplining yourself over and over again — by being honest, being honest, being honest, being honest. Pretty soon, it comes naturally to you. It becomes part of your character, part of your person, and part of your identity.

There's an old adage that says if you want to be happy, practice virtue. It's true. It is old-fashioned, and it works best if you are surrounded by love, warmth, and caring. As the *Harvard Mental Health Letter* said: "The advice inscribed on the Temple of Apollo at Delphi was know yourself, not approve of yourself."

One anecdotal example of the non-relationship between high self-esteem and achievement comes from Harold Stevenson and James Stigler in their book *The Learning Gap*. It is a report on their testing of the elementary school children in Japan, Taiwan, and China, compared with the U.S. The

Asian students, as I am sure you know, far outdistanced the American students — yet, the authors say:

> The Americans exhibited a significantly higher self-evaluation of their academic prowess than their foreign peers. In other words, they combined a lousy performance with a high sense of self-esteem.

For more than twenty years, it has been my joy — as caretaker of Fr. Flanagan's dreams — to throw a spectacular dinner for our girls starting at 1:00 p.m. on Christmas Day. Usually about 40 or 50 girls cannot go home for Christmas, for a variety of reasons. During the first hour, I start off by saying: "Girls, you will all someday be mothers running families and, during this hour today, let us teach you how to make sure there will be happiness on Christmas Day in your future family." Then we go around the room asking what each girl has learned from their bad Christmases so far. Here are some of their answers.

"Don't have drunks or people on drugs over for Christmas Day."

"Don't let people fight constantly. If they do, send them home."

"Don't let Mom and Dad abandon their children on Christmas Day to do partying."

**DISPATCH B**

One of our boys from Kansas City was ordered by a juvenile court judge to do 30 hours of community service. He was to have a court hearing the next Thursday, so he came to me the Friday before and said he needed 20 hours "fast." I told him I could help him, telling him it would be hard work and not fake work. So on Saturday he worked six hours in the garden, and Sunday six hours, and Monday four hours, and four more hours on Tuesday. He started out rather lazy, complaining about the hard work, but I am happy to report he became motivated as he got closer to his 20 hours. He started out as a grump and ended up with a smile on his face, with a good job, well done. He was happy to report, as he stood before the judge, that he had done 20 hours of community service. As we were leaving the court, he said, "I feel a lot better about myself now." A good example of how performance precedes genuine self-esteem.

By this time, the girls can smell the wonderful turkey, dressing, and gravy aromas coming from the kitchen —

so when I ask them what makes a good Christmas, their answers often reflect that connection:

"Make a really good dinner for your children."

"Invite grandma and grandpa over and make them feel welcome."

"Have uncles and aunts."

"Insist that everyone be happy. If they don't, they cannot stay."

"Share stories."

"Do some singing."

"Play games."

Then the real fun begins, when I ask them, "What is the best thing to serve on Christmas?"

The Louisiana girls say, "Gumbo, jambalaya, and crawdads."

The kids from the South say, "Ribs, chicken, ham, and collards."

Others say, "Make sure you spend a long time cooking in the kitchen," or "Don't bring anything from a restaurant. Make it yourself."

What about presents?

"Make sure your kids are happy."

"Don't give them everything they want, but give them more love than they ever needed."

Year after year at this festive gathering, by the time we sit down for dinner, the girls feel good about what they accomplished through their discussion of how a mom can make Christmas happy. It's only after our talk that we have tasty turkey, wonderful dressing, mashed potatoes, piping hot brown gravy, and salads of all kinds.

All this brings to mind the old saying that happiness is like the wake of a ship. It follows those who do not pursue it.

Isn't it interesting that kids for whom life had been hard when they were young almost all came to a crossroads? The road on the right was the road of sacrifices and learning how to be grateful. The road on the left entailed not learning these lessons and getting mired in excuses and learned helplessness. Those who take the road of sacrifice and self-discipline learn how to care for one another and how to bounce back. The key for them is to develop certain virtues within a warm, loving environment — virtues like courage, learning how to be happy and humble, and spunk, or "stick-to-itiveness."

I'd like to share with you the story of our New Orleans kids who, in the wake of Hurricane Katrina, were evacuated from our two Boys Town shelters there. Their first stop was San Antonio. I hopped on a Continental plane, went to Houston, then took another plane to San Antonio and arrived just as our 49 kids and 16 staff were moving into the temporary shelter of an abandoned public school near the Alamo. Can you imagine the chaos? And it was August, as hot as San Antonio gets with no air conditioning. The circumstances of these kids were beyond words; most of them didn't know where their families were at that moment, or if they were even alive.

> ### Dispatch C
>
> Freddy, 25, graduated seven years ago. He has a middle-paying job at $15 an hour making cereal at Kellogg's. He said to me, "I came to Boys Town very ill on five meds. You got me off the meds and showed me how to get a job, keep a job, and make friends. I realize that life is hard, but I now [sic] that God am [sic] good. I feel good. Praise [sic] be the name of the Lord."

These kids had never been out of New Orleans. Before the hurricane, their lives had been traumatized by the dysfunctionality of their own families. Some of these kids never knew their fathers. Some said their fathers were street people and probably perished in the storm. Many were lucky to have even a grandparent — but during and after Hurricane Katrina, these kids didn't know if they even still had Grandma. She had been the sole source of warmth, caring, and firm discipline . . . and they didn't know if she was still alive.

These aren't dumb kids we're talking about. Many of them are quite bright. Many of them can read well, having been taught by Grandma or self-taught. For many, however, school was a place of failure — not because they were dumb but because their schools were not places of learning. Others were in bad schools but had one or two marvelous, exceptional teachers who really cared, and really tried, against overwhelming odds.

You know what? Almost all of these New Orleans kids have a profound moral compass and a deep sense of faith in God passed on to them by grandmothers. In other words, they are children of virtue. They have disciplined themselves in the face of hardships and are eager to pray. They may be cynical about the adult world, but they are not bitter about the good Lord. They know life is hard. They know trouble surrounding their lives comes from evil forces, not the Divine. It's amazing how they search their hearts and find the strength and courage to join hands and move forward. Their self-esteem is based on virtue and the deep-set feeling that, with God's help, they can survive and prosper in chaos. They also have the antennae of street kids — so they can tell when adults are caring, and that's why they respond so well under difficult circumstances. That is virtue. This is appropriate self-esteem. What a lesson for all of us.

Ninah Shokraii says it well:

> Schools must abandon their mindless pursuit of empty self-esteem and return to

the fundamental task of helping students do
their best.

At the beginning of this chapter, we said research shows that people with high self-esteem are happier than those without. Now, perhaps you can understand that people who have high self-esteem but lack virtue may be personally happy, but they make a lot of other people miserable. Bullies lack virtue. High self-esteem bullies are happier than low self-esteem bullies — but they're still bullies!

---

**DISPATCH D**

Akieda is now 22. She told me, "I was in a psychiatric hospital for three years before I came to Boys Town, and the doctor said I would be there for many more years. But you helped me find the courage and the strength to overcome my depression and to learn how to be happy. I may not be a millionaire, but I am happier than many who have so much money." That is healthy self-esteem with lots of virtue.

---

The same sort of dynamic is at play when research shows that people with high self-esteem are more willing to undertake difficult tasks and reenergize themselves when things get tough. That would be true of a high-esteem drug dealer whose market has dried up and who needs to reenergize himself and get a new market for his death-dealing drugs.

Likewise, research suggests that those with self-esteem may holistically leave behind projects that do not work. But think of a high-self-esteem con artist who abandons his schemes when he cannot manipulate others and goes to projects where he can.

Finally, medical evidence suggests self-esteemers even have a lesser danger of heart disease. Big deal. People with high self-esteem who are bullies, drug dealers, and schemers have less danger of heart disease. Somehow that doesn't make a very good case for stand-alone self-esteem!

No, it's the practice of virtue with self-esteem that's the powerful combination. High self-esteem does not promote virtue. Self-esteem without virtue is narcissism, but loving God and your neighbor in word and deed promotes both virtue *and* self-esteem. This is one of the big lessons we've learned when dealing with needy children and families — but it's just as appropriate in your family, too.

# Chapter Five

# The Need for Warmth: Authoritative Communities

*U need 2 no authoritarian parenting duzsnt work n permissive parenting duznt work . . . u need 2 no wat duz.*

You need to know authoritarian parenting doesn't work and permissive parenting doesn't work . . . you need to know what does.

The fifth "dispatch from the front" comes from the base of a cliff. America is standing with ambulances and stretchers at the bottom to pick up our injured youth, but too few people seem concerned about building a fence at the top to prevent our kids from falling. Had I not been so involved with so many children day in and day out for a quarter century, it wouldn't have dawned on me that the mental and behavioral health of America's youngsters is deteriorating in very significant ways. The purpose of this intelligence report is to invite you and others to join together in accident prevention.

Two decades ago, we at Boys Town started a National Hotline for troubled children and families. To this day, we average 800 to 1,000 daily calls from across all fifty states from children and parents in great distress. In one sense, our Hotline is like a gigantic national listening post for hearing the failings, the troubles, and even the sins of America's families and their children. Stories of dysfunctionality, abuse, neglect, suicide, rape, and violence of every kind fill our long lines. Over the years, it is clear to the reflective thinkers among our Hotline counselors that things are not getting better, but worse. The mental and behavioral health of America's children today is rapidly deteriorating. Children are suffering more.

This is not a scare tactic, and it's not a public relations ploy. We know this clinically from our Hotline — but perhaps more importantly, it is also the conclusion of the Commission on Children at Risk (2003), a prestigious panel of 33 research scientists, mental health experts, and youth service professionals brought together by Dartmouth Medical School, The Institute for American Values, and the YMCA of the USA.

Researchers report rising rates of depression, anxiety, conduct disorders, attention deficit, thoughts of suicide, and many other serious behavioral and emotional problems among America's children and adolescents. This includes physical ailments such as asthma, heart disease, irritable bowel syndrome, and ulcers. The Commission on Children at Risk calls this a double crisis — first, a crisis in our children's health; then, a crisis in the way we are responding simply by using psychotherapies and medications.

What has caused this increase to crisis level in the mental and social illness of our children? The Commission says it is a breakdown in what are called authoritative communities: "a lack of connectedness . . . [or] close connections." These professionals are talking about something very fundamental, very basic — a lack of social, structural, and interpersonal warmth and structure in families, schools, and communities. What makes the Commission's finding so important is its scientific base. This is not a group of ideologues, spinning webs of various hypotheses. These people are in the hard sciences of infant attachment and child and adolescent brain development, together with sociologists, describing how society shapes outcomes for children. They are calling for what they see as a desperately needed new model of child development that combines biological and ecological scientific constructs.

---

**DISPATCH A**

Joseph, 16, called our Hotline wanting to end his life, has ingested Benadryl and a great quantity of alcohol. He was vomiting throughout the call. He does not feel he has support in his life. He lives in Manchester, NH, with his mother and his father lives Brookline, MA. Thank goodness he gave us his phone number so the rescue squad could be called.

---

Two kinds of connections need to be built: close connections to other people in family, school, sports, and the community, and "deep connections to moral and spiritual meaning."

But let's go back a step. What are authoritative communities? The Commission defines and explains them this way:

> Groups of people who are committed to one another over time and who model and pass on at least part of what it means to be a good person and live a good life. The weakening of authoritative communities in the U.S. is a principal reason why large and growing numbers of U.S. children are failing to flourish.

The report then gives the following ten main planks of "the new scientific case for authoritative communities."

1. The mechanisms by which we become and stay attached to others are biologically primed and increasingly discernible in the basic structure of the brain.

2. Nurturing environments, or the lack of them, affect gene transcription and the development of brain circuitry.

3. The odd "nature versus nurture" debate — focusing on whether heredity or environment is the main determinant of human conduct — is no longer relevant to serious discussions of child well-being and youth programming.

4. Adolescent risk-taking and novelty-seeking are connected to changes in brain structure and function.

5. Assigning meaning to gender in childhood and adolescence is a human universal that deeply influences well-being.

6. The beginning of morality is the biologically primed moralization of attachment.

7. The ongoing development of morality in later childhood and adolescence involves the human capacity to idealize individuals and ideas.

8. Primary nurturing relationships influence early spiritual development — call it the spiritualization of attachment — and spiritual development can influence us biologically in the same ways that primary nurturing relationships do.

9. Religiosity and spirituality significantly influence well-being.

10. The human brain appears to be organized to ask ultimate questions and seek ultimate answers.

Perhaps an example will help illustrate what the Commission is getting at when they talk about authoritative communities.

Joey comes from a middle-class family of alcohol and drugs. There is constant bickering, backbiting, and fighting and a clear lack of connectedness. No warmth. There is a prevailing spirit of unhappiness, a spirit of "I come first." The kids often get their own meals using the microwave.

When Joey came to us, he was suffering from depression and ADD. He moved into a Boys Town home designed for connectedness, good structure, closeness between people, and openness to moral and spiritual meaning. The home is designed for kindness and caring.

---

### DISPATCH B

Elizabeth, 13, called stating she has been sexually abused repeatedly by her older brother and is afraid to tell her parents. When we tried to connect her with Child Protective Services in a small town in Southern Missouri, she hung up. Through National Call Locator, we called back and were able to have her talk with the sheriff's office and then Project Harmony.

---

That does not mean that solely kindness and caring are there 24 hours a day. Of course, there is bickering and fighting, but it is occasional, not constant. It happens now and then. The focus is on teaching skills and building positive, caring relationships. Gradually, slowly but surely, Joey is beginning to get better . . . with less reliance on medications . . . now, even without individual therapy.

You can sometimes do the same in your own homes. We can do the same in our schools and churches. What is needed? Good closeness between the people living in the home, good closeness between the school's teachers and students (like a family), and good closeness in our churches.

Joey has been living in what the National Commission calls an authoritative community, one that is both preventive and therapeutic. It is a home here in the Village of Boys Town. You can create the same wherever you live. The Village has a warm environment and everyone here is dedicated to providing firm moral guidance with warmth. In this environment, there are three generations who care and share and where moral teaching is predominant — the kids, the Family-Teachers, the schoolteachers (young and old), the police, the firemen, the maintenance people, and the pastors. The National Commission has utilized the terminology of Diana Baumrind (1966) that we saw in Chapter 2. Like Baumrind's authoritative parenting, an authoritative community includes families, schools, churches, sports leagues, and community. "Authoritative" is just the opposite of either authoritarian or permissive. The purpose of building authoritative communities is to stem the deteriorating of the mental and behavioral health of America's children. Its purpose is to help children grow up mentally, behaviorally, and spiritually healthy.

That's how it began to slowly dawn on Joey that his days didn't have to be filled with depression; that life could be good; and that he was put on this earth for a purpose. He was not just the result of some sperm and ovum that aimlessly bumped into each other one day. This "good life" is a matter of family, schools, churches, sports, recreation, and so many adults pulling together. Joey learns basic skills here, such as how to follow instructions, how to accept negative feedback, how to take no for answer, how to disagree appropriately, and many others. He receives firm guidance in the midst of kindness and caring.

---

**DISPATCH C**

Janine, 10, calls almost every day from Bremerton, WA. Her mother is an RN in a local hospital working the 3-to-11 shift, and when Janine comes home after school, she just likes to call and talk to someone because she is home all alone. We love to hear from her, and Janine always says, "You are my friends. I like to talk to you."

---

The National Commission lists ten characteristics of an authoritative community that we strive to provide at the Village of Boys Town, but you can create the same wherever you live. These are the ten characteristics:

1. It is a large social body that includes children and youth.

2. It treats children as ends in themselves.

3. It's warm and nurturing.

4. It establishes clear limits and expectations.

5. The core of its work is performed largely by non-specialists.

6. It's multi-generational.

7. It has a long-term focus.

8. It reflects and transmits a shared understanding of what it means to be a good person.

9. It encourages spiritual and religious development.

10. It's philosophically oriented to the equal dignity of all persons and to the principle of love of neighbor.

To put it simply, if we can bring warmth and firm structure — along with psychological autonomy and moral guidance — to bear on our children through daily teaching of skills via family, churches, schools, sporting organizations, and social recreation, then fewer children will have mental health problems and the need for pharmacology and individual therapy will decrease.

This latter point is more important than many realize. The report clearly says that while we as a nation are making significant progress in the area of individual treatment with psychotropic drugs and therapy, at the same time, more kids are getting sick. We're helping more kids at the bottom of the cliff who have already fallen off, but we're not diminishing the number of kids at the top who are close to the edge. We have ambulances below to pick up those who are hurt, but no fences at the top of the cliff. *In other words, we are regressing in the area of prevention.*

A good example of regressing is the issue of school dropouts and what to do about them. You can simply look at individual boys and girls and try to help those who have dropped out, which is the way most of America deals with the problem now. Or you can look at the serious problems of schools and families and fix them so fewer and fewer kids drop out. In addition, the report says that the "at-risk" model of looking at children has very serious limitations because it focuses on individuals. It largely fails to look at the social and family setting that is precipitating these problems — namely, the lack of authoritative communities. As *Washington Post* columnist William Raspberry put it:

> The [coal] miners who once used canaries, with their fragile respiratory systems, to warn of toxicity in the mines understood that it wasn't enough to distribute gas masks to individuals, but that it was important to do something about the environment in which those individuals labored.
>
> Our focus, unfortunately, has been on providing artificial respiration for gasping canaries.[1]

Schools aren't alone in this. The troubles currently afflicting the Christian churches in America, including our own Roman Catholic Church, come to mind as well.

---

[1] William Raspberry, "Environmentally Challenged." *The Washington Post*, Sept. 22, 2003. http://www.cmresearch.org/resources/kids/newspaper_articles/2005/030505_raspberry.htm.

It's clear that the evidence suggests human beings are hardwired for meaning; i.e., biologically driven both by relationships and questions such as *What's it all about? What is life? What is the meaning of it all?* The Commission puts it this way:

> Children's moral and spiritual needs are as genuine and as integral to their personhood as their physical and intellectual needs.

And also:

> The beginning of morality is the biologically primed moralization of attachment.

Let me share a small example from my own life. Eleven-year-old Hanna had been having bad dreams about someone coming to kill her family, one by one, and then searching for her. The environment in which she and her mom lived was filled with noonday terrors and evil creatures of the night. Her world was lacking positive meaning and needed to be charged with affirming meaning — a need that, if the Commission is correct, is biologically driven. After she had been with us for about three months, I showed Hanna how to get rid of this bad monster of the night. I told her to kneel down every night by her bed, sprinkle holy water on the four corners of the bed, and when she slowly says the Lord's Prayer, to listen to God the Father in heaven saying two things to her. First, "You are my princess." Second, "I will protect you. I have sent someone." I told her that we were that someone.

The next week when I saw her, she said, "I said the prayer and hopped into bed. Then I saw in the dark the hooded figure coming toward me. I prayed to my Father, used more holy water, and He chased him away. I do this every night and it works."

I've simplified the story a little, but it shows how warmth in authoritative parenting is essential.

It's important to notice the kind of warmth we are talking about. Warmth is sometimes mistakenly equated with permissive parenting, a kind of "anything goes" attitude. But in terms of a child's growth and development, permissive parenting is equivalent to neglectful parenting. On the other hand, the warmth we are talking about is not authoritarian ("I will beat the becheebers out of you for love of you"), either. This is using the word *warmth* without communicating anything other than punishment. The warmth we are talking about is authoritative warmth: namely, "warm and involved, as well as firm in establishing guidelines, limits, and expectations." Research shows that authoritative parenting correlates with very good behavioral, psychological, and spiritual outcomes for children.

It is important to understand this distinction between authoritative warmth and permissive warmth. Why? Because they work in different ways. If permissive parents want children simply to feel good about themselves, then there is no need to grow up, to tackle developmental challenges, to bring a person to a higher level of caring, sharing, and adult happiness. Do you really want your children to have high self-esteem, to always "feel good about themselves" even when they have lied, cheated, and stolen? If that is the goal, then they will never grow up. And if always feeling good about themselves is a parent's goal for a child, then mom or dad are not helping their children gain self-respect, respect of others, and a good moral compass.

> **DISPATCH D**
>
> Armando says he is filled with pain. He feels everybody leaves him. He said his own parents deserted him. He has a long history of feelings of abandonment. His father said he did not want him in his home. He now lives with an uncle in the same town as his father. He cried throughout much of the Hotline call. His mental and behavioral health is deteriorating rapidly.

Even authoritarian parents can have out-of-control children. Their hardnosed approach, coupled with lack of warmth, can produce depression, loneliness, resentment, and sometimes, more opposition and defiance. Other parents have been permissive, and their children are equally out of control. Many parents in these circumstances are convinced that the only effective strategy available at this point is to make sure their children are safe.

But what does "safe" mean? Consider the man in Harrison, New York, who rented three hotel rooms for his son and his friends on New Year's Eve 2002, so they would be "safe" while ringing in the New Year. Police made 26 arrests for alcohol and drugs. But the family said, "At least they were safe."

---

### DISPATCH E

Leah, 11, came from a background of sadness, cold indifference, cynicism, and craftiness in her acutely dysfunctional family. She walked slowly into her Boys Town home with sad brown eyes, a cheap dirty dress, unkempt hair, and low-grade depression. It took a while for her to so much as smile. What started her smiling was the very affectionate family dog, Daisy, who would not take no for an answer. And on her third day here, her Family-Teacher made her favorite meal. Through relationships with firm structure and caring discipline, Leah was provided an environment of positive affect and a sense of relationship.

---

Or take the 1997 Marilyn Manson concert in the District of Columbia, which featured a quiet room for parents who accompanied their children. "Each time a teenager was wheeled past the room from the mosh pit to the first aid station, the parents raced to the door to make sure the afflicted was not theirs."[2]

You and I can do much better than this. We can bring warmth, structure, discipline, and love to our children. We can bring security and protection to those who are in need of it, and we can help our adolescent children grow up. We can help our churches, our schools, and our communities become the kind of places that help our adolescent children grow up. I have seen what happens when we create, or do not create, authoritative homes and communities. The time to act is now.

---

[2] Diana West, *The Death of the Grown-up: How America's Arrested Development Is Bringing Down Western Civilization* (NY: St. Martin's Griffin, 2008), p. 75.

# CHAPTER SIX

# Resilience

———◦———

*U need 2 no wat r the keyz that make ur kidz resilient.*

You need to know what are the keys that make your kids resilient.

Marty, 10, came to us as a ward of a neighboring state. He was with us eight days when his very nutty state caseworker changed her mind and said he should leave Boys Town and go to foster care. But before he could go to foster care, the psychiatrist ordered an evaluation. So Marty was sent to the emergency ward of a large local hospital, where the emergency room doc said he needed inpatient treatment immediately. Unfortunately, there was no room on the child psychiatric ward so — believe it or not — he lived in the emergency room for three days. The nurses and doctors were very professional, but they had neither the time nor the inclination to surround him with loving attention. The loneliness of those days was nothing more than a prolongation of the loneliness of his eight prior placements. Marty doesn't have resilience; it's not hard to figure out why.

Pierre's father was killed in an accident when he was three, and his mother died of kidney disease was he was five. So his godmother, the lady who held him up in baptism as an infant, welcomed him into her home with her husband

and became like a second mother to him. With warmth, she cared for his many needs, taught him trust, and at the same time set limits for him and showed him the right way to do things. She meant the world to him. When Pierre was eleven, his godmother became very, very ill. He was never quite sure what it was, but she lay in bed week after week as the doctors didn't seem to know what was wrong. One gray, cold winter afternoon he was next door playing with the neighbor kids when was told his godmother wanted to see him. Pierre was scared, but he went to her side right away.

As he sat on her bed, she said weakly, "Pierre, I want you to promise me that no matter what happens you will remember the love I have given you as your godmother, and that you will always be a good boy. You need to promise me that." Pierre said he made that promise with tears in his eyes. Then he added, "My godmother closed her eyes and laid her head on the pillow, and I thought she was sleeping. My whole world came to an end when I realized that she was not breathing. Every day for a year following her death, my stepfather and I ate supper in silence together. All meaning had gone out of my life. I felt numb." Then his stepfather married another woman who had neither the time nor the interest to deal with Pierre. However, his friend down the street had a caring mom and dad. He spent so many nights there that eventually his stepfather gave him permission to move in with them. That family slowly helped Pierre heal, and he became like a son to them.

Pierre is a grownup now, a success as a husband, father, and businessman. When people hear his story and ask him how and why he didn't give up and throw his life away, he talks about his godmother and the neighbors down the street. Pierre is resilient.

At this point, if you're feeling a bit depressed about the state of the American family, this sixth "dispatch from the front" is much more positive. It's about resilience. It's about the reasons why some youth experience huge troubles and trauma and, instead of tanking, work through and overcome these obstacles on the road to success. Its purpose is to encourage parents, teachers, and church workers to help develop resilience in their children.

One of the major elements predictive of resilience is the presence of at least one or two warm, caring relationships. If we want to develop resilience in our children, we need to make sure that they have one or two people — usually family members — who will be close to them in frequent contact for long periods of time; who will love them, be worthy of their trust, hold them accountable, and help them when they are in need.

Is it a coincidence that the research on successful resiliency calls for parent figures with warmth and love on one hand and firm tolerances on the other? No, It's not surprising that this independent research comes up with the same elements we call authoritative parenting. Amazing!

In 1995, a group from the Bernard VonLeer Foundation in Holland published a study on resilience (The International Resilience Research Project) having surveyed more than 1,200 families and children from 27 sites in 22 countries, many of which were war-torn places around the globe, in Africa, the Caucasus, the Middle East and Asia where you would not expect resilience to flourish. In the midst of these horrible circumstances of civil war, ethnic cleansing, religious strife, famine, and disease, why did some children survive and grow strong and others languish and even die?

The study identified three sources of resilience: relationships, attitudes/behaviors, and skills.

The first source of resilience they identified was relationships. We have already spoken about that above. This means stable people in children's lives who see them every day and love them for years and years, whom they can count on and turn to, who regularly hold them accountable and help them overcome adversity.

The researchers found five items statistically significant and indicative of the promise of resilience. When you read them, you may smile a smile of recognition. We have talked about them already. The five are:

- I have people around me I trust who love me no matter what.

- I have people who set limits for me so I know when to stop before there is danger or trouble.

- I have people who show me how to do things right by the way they do things.

- I have people who want me to learn to do things on my own.

- I have people who help me when I am sick, in danger, or need to learn.

If we wish to inculcate resilience in our children, we have to be these people. We have to be authoritative parents.

Looking at these five conditions for resilience (and authoritative parenting), it is easy to see how they function in our faith relationship with the Lord, who remarkably resembles an authoritative parent:

- I am daily close to the Lord, whom I trust and who loves me no matter what.

- I have the Lord in my life, who sets limits for me so I know when to stop before there is danger or trouble.

- I have the Lord Jesus, who shows me how to do things right by the way he did things in his earthly life.

- I have the Lord, who, as Good Shepherd, pushes me to learn to do things on my own with his grace that strengthens me.

- I can turn to the Lord for help when I am sick, in danger, or need to learn.

The Resilience Research Project also identified a second source of resilience: namely, attitudes and behaviors that help a youngster develop into a hopeful kind of person, self-disciplined, self-governed, and capable of self-control. These attitudes and behaviors are a combination of love and self-discipline and represent the basic virtues of family life:

- I am a person people can like and love.

- I am glad to do nice things for others and show my concern.

- I am respectful of myself and others. (I do not lie, cheat, steal, do drugs and alcohol, or tolerate people who do.)

- I am willing to be responsible for what I do.

- I am sure things will be all right.

Remember, there is a difference between reality and appearances here. At one of our open AA meetings, Jodi said it straightforwardly:

> A lot of kids come here to accept a six-month chip on Chip Night, but they drank last week. It's just a front. My mom was a good example. She said she was sober for six and a half years, but I knew it was a front. I would take a drink of her coffee and there was clearly vodka in that coffee. You can tell when people are not sincere.

It is important to help our children see that there are certain behaviors that make them likeable, such as doing nice things for others and showing compassion and concern. And then there are certain behaviors that make it hard for people to love us, or even just like us. If we lie, cheat, and steal on a regular basis, it is very hard for people to like us or trust us.

A good example of concern for others occurred not long ago when, at 10:00 in the morning, a supervisor called to say that 14-year-old Danny's mom had died of a drug overdose the night before and someone needed to tell him. Danny's mom had been a street person in Los Angeles for a long time. His aunt met me, and we went together to see Danny. When the other seven boys in his Boys Town home wanted to go up to the gym, I said, "No, we are going to need you, so please just go out and sit on the porch." When his aunt and I told Danny about his mother, he cried. The tears were of great sadness at losing his mom, but also they were tears of relief that she would now be released from the addiction that kept driving her on to her own destruction. He knew in his heart that his mom would never get better. We talked and prayed together. Then I went outside and had the other seven boys come in. They each came up and gave him a big bear hug and said they were sorry. This is how a band of brothers expresses condolences. It surely helped Danny — but, in my own heart of hearts, I know it also helped the other seven boys become more hopeful persons. What they did is not everything, but it sure helped Danny in developing resilience.

Many of our children come from parents who exercised their individualistic freedom to do "their own thing" and left their children alone and abandoned. Consider, for example, Gina, who was abandoned as a newborn infant in a bassinet in the airport at Reno, Nevada. She was taken by two Continental airline pilots to Lost and Found, where she began her young life among the abandoned luggage. As she grew, she had a choice to either develop attitudes and behaviors that make her a hopeful, resilient person or simply to repeat the abandonment of her parents over and over again.

Our kids know that the option to do your own thing and abandon others is always available, but they also know it won't make them happy. And once they can learn to do nice things for others, to be respectful of others, to be responsible and let others love them, then they start being kids of resilience and hope.

The third source of resilience, according to The Resilience Research Project, is a certain set of skills that a person has mastered that are, at heart, problem-solving skills. The Resilience Research Project lists five that mirror the hoped-for results of authoritative parenting:

- I can talk to others about things that frighten me or bother me.

- I can find ways to solve problems that I face.

- I can control myself when I feel like doing something not right or dangerous.

- I can figure out when it is a good time to talk to someone or take action.

- I can find someone to help me when I need it.

Once a month, we have open sobriety meetings. Kids receive a 3-month, 6-month, or 12-month chip for sobriety and tell their stories. Because they are so encouraging, I'd like to share two of them with you.

My mother and father met many summers ago through their druggie friend. They partied together for several years and ended up getting pregnant. As I was growing up in South Florida, I got the message you could use, have fun, and live life like a normal druggie person. So I started using and having fun, and drugs became my only friend. Drugs were there in good times and in bad. Drugs were loyal and definitely got the job done, but I was hooked. I had no desire to get better, and I never began the road to recovery until I came here to Boys Town. You surrounded me with caring people who set limits for me and who helped me trust them. You helped me learn some self-respect and friendship skills. And above all, you taught me that there is a Higher Power and if I trust the Lord, I can stay sober one day at a time.

— Martha

I thank the Lord for being sober for 2½ years. I know it makes me a stronger person. It is not easy every day, for every time I am upset I have that feeling I could really use a beer right now. I have learned to rely on others when I want to drink, and they help me find success. I thank those for helping with my sobriety one day at a time.

— John, 17

How does a person gain the skills they need for resilience? Again, I'd like to let some resilient kids tell you in their own words. These children are very ill and are in our Boys Town hospital. I asked them how they gained the resiliency skills that they need; here are some of their answers — answers that show them building resilience as part of their character:

> When I came here to the hospital, I refused to wake up in the morning, but you helped me gain self-control and now I am the first one up, ready to go and happy.
>
> — Regina

A small skill, a small step in the right direction.

> I didn't know impulse control when I came and the staff are so good they taught me how to take deep breaths and other things that work. Now I feel better.
>
> — George

This is a tougher skill, harder to learn.

> I learned from my grandmother that if I want to come home, I will have to put in a lot of hard work here at the hospital, and there are people helping me learn the skills I need.
>
> — Marty

Finally, I'd like to share with you the story of one of our lads, Edgar, who is into Wicca (spells, incantations, black magic, power and control, hatred, anger, and frustration).

He has been in 14 (yes, 14) placements; he says people told him they would love him, but they didn't. So now he has given up on goodness and love and is embracing badness and hatred. He likes the feeling of power it gives him over others.

So I asked him, "Edgar, where are you going to go when we have to dismiss you?"

Tears came to his eyes for the first time. "Father, this is the only good home I have ever had. I don't want to leave."

"Well, then, Edgar," I told him, "if you are in a good home, you have to put away your hatred and your bitterness. Think it over."

The next day, he came back to me and said slowly, "Well, I guess I am ready to dump Wicca, but I don't know how." I told him that we would help him and that he could do it. Every day, slowly but surely, Edgar is gaining the skills, attitudes, and relationships he needs to make the break. It's not easy, and he has to do it in stages, by pulling and twisting and turning.

Resilience is like planting a cucumber patch. It takes time, patience, hard work, and perseverance, even re-planting if the spring rains wash it all out. But we hope these stories are an encouragement to parents, educators, and church workers, because raising kids to be resilient is one of the best gifts we can give our children — yours and mine alike.

CHAPTER SEVEN

# God and Morality

———◦◦◦———

*U need 2 no kids r like u in their vu of god, but not like u in morality.*

You need to know kids are like you in their view of God, but not like you in morality.

The seventh "dispatch from the front" may seem counterintuitive, because it is about young people's religious beliefs and moral values and practices. Something of a paradox is at work here. Many are convinced that both the religious beliefs and the morals of young people differ greatly from their parents, but the facts show a more complicated picture. Yes, there is a massive disconnect between the moral values and practices of parents and young people in the area of lying, cheating, stealing, and sexually acting out, and you can throw churchgoing into that mix as well. However, no such gigantic disconnect exists between the religious beliefs of parents and young people. To put it simply, although the moral *behavior* of the children has deteriorated and has become far different from the morals of their parents, the *beliefs* of both parents and children are approximately the same. The culture has a stranglehold on the minds and hearts of many teenagers in moral practices. Let us then see how we can teach our kids to be different from the toxic culture that bombards them 24/7.

Much research shows that religious commentators who say kids today are inclined toward New Age quests and Eastern religious experiences, very much like hippies of the '60s and '70s, are quite wrong. Kids today are very conventional in their view of God. Interestingly enough, for many, many teenagers, the God they believe in resembles what we have already earlier called a permissive parent!

How does this work? If God is like a permissive parent, then God looks like someone who brought you into the world, loves you warmly and caringly, suggests you be kind and not rip each other off, and gives you as much

### DISPATCH A

Before I came to Boys Town, I had no faith in God because my family had no faith. Here, all the adults are people of faith, so I have started to follow them to church and get involved in church-related activities. My faith has started to grow. I have a lot better faith in God now. I remember once a friend at work asked me if I wanted to smoke weed. I had the courage to say no. God has faith in us and we have to put faith in him. When we do, we have the strength to make life a lot better.

— Nicole, 15

freedom as possible by not getting involved a lot in your personal life. A teen with a permissive mom or dad likes the idea that, in some ways, their mom and dad keep at a safe distance — and thinks that God acts in a similar fashion.

The 2004 National Study on Youth and Religion confirms this concept of God among American teenagers. It's very similar to the belief in theism, predominant among the founding fathers of our Republic. Theism believes in a God who is creator, designer of the universe, giver of moral guidelines, kindly disposed toward humanity, and non-Trinitarian. In other words, Jesus and the Holy Spirit are not part of this idea of God. God is sort of like the clockmaker of Deism, who made the universe like a very large clock and lets it tick and tock on its own.

However, today's teens attribute a second characteristic to God that differs from traditional theism: a therapeutic role. This means that God is available when you are sick; in trouble with the police, the law, or school; or when a tragedy happens, such as a friend committing suicide or being killed in an auto accident, or when you're feeling bad about a breakup with your girlfriend or boyfriend. For teens, God is a loving parent who shows up in those circumstances — or a sensitive counselor who will listen caringly and lend a hand in grief management or a candlelight vigil.

If teenagers' view of God is a permissive parent, often that view mirrors their parents' idea of God as well. Mom and Dad say that God is important in their own lives, but not centrally important. Religion is not the primary organizing principle of either teens' or parents' lives — nor the central source of energy, nor the central goal setter, but they feel God is to be relied on in crises. Even though God may have rules about sex, drugs, and alcohol, in this view they are not too strictly enforced. Love of God and service of neighbor are important to a teen, but other things are more important. For boys, the more important things are sports, grooming, and girls. For girls, the more important things are shopping, grooming, and boys. Finally, they believe there may be a heaven, but surely not a hell.

Our secular society finds this permissive-parenting notion of God quite acceptable and wants religion to stay mostly in the private sphere, making no public moral demands and appearing in public only for such ritual events as inaugurations and state funerals. Our secular culture also embraces the therapeutic notion that God is there to help when we are in trouble or need. God is good, loving, and not very demanding. The influence of our culture is one big reason why moralistic, therapeutic theism is so prevalent in our children: our churches and parents hold pretty much to the same view.

As previously mentioned, in 2004, the Lilly Endowment funded a research project titled the National Study of Youth and Religion. In it, researchers and scholars hoped to answer many questions. Is religion, especially among American youth, very diverse and pluralistic, especially with the new immigrants coming from Asia with their Eastern religions, or is Christianity still the mainstream? Are young people alienated from their parents' religion? Are they turning away from traditional religion? Have they been impacted by society's sexual revolution? Have they been touched by the drug culture? Is alcohol a more serious problem?

The National Study of Youth and Religion summarizes its findings in eleven recurrent general themes. Let us look at each of them and see how they are helpful to understanding our children today.

---

### DISPATCH B

People here at Boys Town passed on their faith to me. What I learned is that by faith we can see God's hand in our lives. Without faith, we can't see it. When you have faith, you can see the spirit of God working. When I was baptized, I saw my life changing in many ways. It is kind of hard to write about what I see. You can see what you have sacrificed to be happy in the long run. You can look back and tell yourself that you have chosen wisely. God opens our eyes to see good and evil when we believe and gives us the strength to do good. To me, I see more of the meaning of life and my purpose in life.

— Jimmy, an eighth-grader

DISPATCH C

Before I came here, I lived in a broken home full of broken promises that were either made to me by parents or that I made to others. I was into depression and my depression led to anger. I counted on myself to deal with the pain. I dug a hole and felt there was no way out. I tried music and when it lost touch with me, I had nothing. When I got here, I didn't want to be in the hole I found myself in, so I picked myself up and started digging myself out. This was due to my Family-Teachers. Without them, I could not be successful. They showed me how to get in touch with the Lord. This little town has shown me that I can be a good friend to others and has given me some of the best friends I thought I would never have. It has shown me how a true family works and how faith works.

— Christina, 16

1) **Religion is a significant presence in the lives of many U.S. teens today.**

Our experience here in the Village of Boys Town tends to bear this out, in the sense that religion was not a significant presence for many of our youth upon entry, but it is not difficult for them to see the benefits of involvement in conventional religion and assimilate this once they experience those therapeutic benefits. When boys and girls come to our Village, they become part of a home where a married couple role-models family skills, academic skills, and religious skills. Outside of Boys Town, the same will be true as long as you have one or two good adult role models, namely, mom, dad, grandmother, or grandfather who role-model these same skills.

2) **Contrary to many popular assumptions and stereotypes, the character of teenage religiosity in the United States is extraordinarily conventional.**

This study of 3,290 teens ages 13-17 shows the vast majority express religious moralistic and therapeutic beliefs that are remarkably similar to the generation before them. This should not surprise us because it is a truism that most children have followed their parents' religious views in the past, so we would expect the same today. If there is no practice of religion with parents, there is none with children. If there is little religiosity with parents, there is usually next to none with children. Our founder, Fr. Flanagan, said over and over again: "There are no bad boys. There is only bad environment, bad training, bad example, and bad thinking."

When there is no religiosity found in their immediate family, however, we at Boys Town can almost guarantee that an appeal to grandmother will bring about happy results.

> **DISPATCH D**
>
> Before I came here, I was headed down the same path everyone in my family took . . . no faith, no hope, no love. No one in the neighborhood graduated from high school where I grew up. I didn't care that what I was doing was wrong. I hated going to school. I would go out drinking with my friends and get into fights. During my time here, my mom got sick and died. I knew I was going to lose her. She fell into a coma. I turned to the Lord and although she died, it changed everything. It was my Family-Teachers taking my parents' place who hung in with me and my pastor. They loved me. They helped me dream a dream and live that dream. I now have a future I never thought I would have.
>
> — Amanda, 15

Joey is a good example. When I asked him, "What religion do you practice?" He answered, "None."

I asked, "How about your mom and dad?"

"None."

"What about your grandmother?"

"My grandmother is a Baptist."

"Then, Joey, you are a Baptist."

Joey smiled a smile of recognition. He said, "How do you know this?"

I said, "Just ask your grandmother. She will be happy to tell you."

Almost all our kids are like Joey.

3) **Very few U.S. youth younger than the age of 18 appear to be exposed to, interested in, or actively pursuing the kind of "spiritual, but not religious" personal quests of eclectic spiritual seeking about which we have heard so much lately.**

Some adults may be on a religious quest of this kind or that kind, and many media stars glorify this approach to life, but it is clear to us here at Boys Town that the NSYR study is right on.

Philosophers and developmental psychologists have sometimes argued that once the basic needs for food and shelter and the other fundamental essentials have been met, there is an automatic quest for something more. This view fails to take into account the fact that as long as the entertainment media in our culture is wholly encompassing, all else may be postponed. It seems for many American teens that if they are sufficiently entertained, a further religious quest beyond that of their parents is not an urgent one.

4) **Comparing statistics over time shows that the religiodemographic diversity represented by U.S. adolescents is no more varied today than it has been for a very long time.**

The vast majority of teenagers today, when asked, identify themselves as Christians; those who do not, identify themselves as Mormon, Jewish, or non-religious. Only a small number identify themselves as Hindu, Buddhist, Wiccan, or the like.

5) **It is Mormon teenagers who are faring the best sociologically. After Mormon youth, conservative Protestant and black Protestant teenagers who score the next highest on most sociological indicators. Mainline Protestant teens come next in religious strength, and are followed by a poor showing of Catholic, Jewish, and non-religious teenagers. Why do the Catholic youth score so low?**

The study points to "upward mobility, mainstream acculturation, and declining religious strength in twentieth-century U.S. Catholicism." In the past, Catholics were historically regarded as dangerous outsiders and of lower economic status. As outsiders, they tended to stick together and show pride (as outsiders) in who they were with regular Sunday Mass attendance, living up to Catholic morality, and embracing many Catholic devotional practices. Today, many upwardly mobile Catholic teens do not find their religious status as strongly identifying themselves as different and apart from others. The culture has triumphed in this regard. They are just like everybody else. In addition, the study suggests that the relatively lower Catholic teenage religiosity may be due somewhat to general demographic factors of lower religiosity: Catholic teenagers tend to be more likely to reside in the Northeast, a generally less religious region of the country.

6) **The evidence clearly shows that the single most important social influence on the religious and spiritual lives of adolescents is their parents.**

Speaking of how children resemble their parents, the study says parents "will get what they are." That is well said.

7) **Our findings suggest a significant supply-side dynamic operating in the religious and spiritual lives of U.S. teenagers. It appears that the greater the supply of religiously grounded relationships, activities, programs, opportunities, and challenges available for teenagers, other things being equal, the more likely teenagers will be religiously engaged and invested.**

Some time ago, U.S. Supreme Court Justice Clarence Thomas came to town, and some of our kids were lucky enough to go listen to him. During the question and answer period, one of our African-American kids from Mississippi raised his hand and asked, "Mr. Justice, did you ever have any troubles like I have when you were growing up?" Justice Thomas answered:

> Yes. I had many, many troubles . . . big ones . . . when growing up in the South, but I had people of faith who surrounded me and helped me to grow through my troubles with the grace of God. Now, I look on those

troubles of my childhood as one of the best blessings I ever had.

8) **At the level of subjective consciousness, adolescent religious and spiritual understanding and concern seem to be generally very weak.**

Just as there is a huge deficit in our children's understanding of American history, so is there a huge deficit of their understanding of the gospels, the Apostles' Creed, the sacraments, the liturgy and the prayer life of the Church. The study says it this way:

> For very many U.S. teens, religion is important, but not a priority, valued but not much invested; praised, but not very describable.

In the minds of teenagers, the ecumenism of Vatican II has watered down Catholicism to such an extent that religion is generally a nice and helpful thing to have, but that's all. I recall giving marriage instructions to a very young couple, and the potential groom in one session was markedly fidgeting. Finally, when I asked him about it, he said, "I came here to get married, not to get religion."

9) **A particular religious outlook that is distinct from the traditional faith commitments of most historical U.S. religious traditions, what we are calling Moralistic Therapeutic Deism, appears to have established a significant foothold among very many contemporary U.S. teenagers.**

We spoke about this earlier in this chapter. This, of course, would be less true among Mormon youth or conservative Protestant and black Protestant teenagers. It is much more prevalent among mainline Protestant teens and Catholic teenagers. This does not mean, for example, that Catholic religious educators necessarily promote this. *What it does mean is that teenagers mainly turn to God in times of tragedy, suffering, and pain.* For anyone who has been at a funeral in our churches lately, there is a very therapeutic moralistic theme, namely, that God is very good and loving and is welcoming just about everybody to heaven.

10) **It is not sufficient to focus only on teenagers' individual psychological issues or moral character, or smart or poor choices and behaviors; those are often themselves shaped powerfully by the social and cultural forces of therapeutic individualism, mass-consumer capitalism, the digital communication revolution, residual positivism and empiricism, the structural disconnect of teenagers from the world of adults' own problems, and other relevant cultural and social contradictions and tensions.**

This is a rather complicated way of saying that the influences of the larger culture, especially adolescent-focused advertising, music, DVDs, and the whole entertainment industry, have a huge impact on teenagers. Christian moral teaching is a minor influence. In days gone by, the effect of a toxic culture was to some degree mitigated by school, church, community, extended family, and neighborhood. Not so today. Consumer society affects both parents and children, as do mass consumer capitalism,

> **DISPATCH E**
>
> I learned with the help of Barb, my Family-Teacher, who has great faith, to see good in tough situations. She helped me to realize that when I run into a brick wall that a turning point in my life has occurred. She tells me the turning point is bringing me one step closer to God's plan for me and God is there to help me. I don't see it as a punishment anymore. I have faith in my hard times.
>
> — Heather, 16

practical materialism, the whole new digital communication world, and narcissistic individualism. The teen culture — the anger, loneliness, frustration, and the drugs, sex, and alcohol — create a massive disconnect. Religion is a marginal player in this regard; this cannot be overemphasized.

Let me give you an example.

Ian is from a well-to-do family on Manhattan's Upper West Side. Four generations ago, his great-grandparents immigrated to this country from Europe, bringing with them almost no material goods, but a reservoir of deep-rooted faith and a desire for a better life. Through hard work, perseverance, and the strength of their family and their church, their children prospered.

By the time their grandchildren came along, they no longer spoke Czech. They had risen economically and felt very much a part of the American mainstream. Young Ian's identity was shaped, not by his faith or Czech ancestry, but by upper-middle-class values of individualism, consumerism, and the practical materialism he shares with his mom and dad. They are really nice people, but unable to manage or cope successfully with Ian's toxic youth culture of anger and drugs, loneliness and sex, frustration and alcohol. That is why he came to us with typical intake adolescent characteristics imbedded in his life: truancy, failing grades, lying, cheating, stealing, drugs, sex, and alcohol. *His views of God and religion are remarkably similar to his mom and dad,* but the disconnect between his youth culture and their adult culture gives the mistaken impression his view of God and religion is another disconnect. It is not. This disconnect is moral — not happenstance — and massive.

11) **We observe sizeable and significant differences in a variety of important life outcomes between more or less religious teenagers in the United States. Highly religious teenagers appear to be doing much better in life than less religious teenagers. We believe the empirical evidence suggests that religious faith and practice themselves exert significant, positive, direct, and indirect influences on the lives of teenagers, helping to foster healthier, more engaged adolescents who live more constructive and promising lives. Most teenagers don't insist that religion is good for people for no reason at all.**

The findings of the NSYR study resonate with what we know from years and years of experience here at Boys Town dealing with children whom life has failed not at the end, not at the middle, but at the very beginning. Teenagers who have strong religious faith are better equipped to deal with powerful social and cultural forces of our society that, in an age of permissive parenting, have even more force and persuasion.

Today, marketing and public relations have developed techniques so powerfully subtle that kids can be persuaded to adopt hedonistic politically-correct views on moral issues without ever realizing this is happening to them. In our world, the individual is manipulated through techniques of persuasion more powerful than ever in the history of advertising. These techniques are so well developed that

> **DISPATCH F**
>
> In the Bronx where I grew up, I never heard of Holy Week. My family never participated in it or in any religion. I never ever went to church and I never prayed because they did not either. All of that changed when I came to Boys Town. I know what it means to pray. Now, I know what it feels like to go to church and understand the passion, death and resurrection of Jesus and the part they play in my life.
>
> — Juan, 17

individuals are sold a bill of goods unawares; in many instances, this accounts for the massive disconnect between parents and children. If that is true in so many normal families, how true it must be in very dysfunctional families?

We see this all the time here at Boys Town. We know from experience that without solid faith underpinnings of authoritative parenting, our Boys Town children are being swept out to sea on a tide of despair, alienation, loneliness, bitterness, sex, drugs, and alcohol. Cultural conditioning is that powerful. Whether we like it or not, there is a war against our children and families being waged by the forces of abuse, neglect, alienation, dysfunctionality, divorce, suicide, gangs, and violence on one hand — and on the other hand, by a culture that says this is the way life is and we need to accept it. If our youth do not get in touch with our Christian faith and morality, as traditionally understood, and use it as a much more powerful counterforce, then they are powerless before these terrible forces in their lives. *That makes it even more important that the triangle of authoritative parenting, authoritative communities, and authoritative religious teaching join together in a coalition to nurture healthier, stronger adolescents to live more constructive and promising lives.*

We have learned at Boys Town from long experience that our religious heritage can be passed on and that teenagers can embrace it. It is a big mistake to think that teenagers today mirror religious convictions of the hippy generation of the 1960s and 1970s. All of our experience shows that this is simply not true. It is a mistake to think otherwise.

But it's also a mistake to think that our teenagers can not be taught to see through all the postmodern lies of our advertising age. Our children need to be Christianized. This simply means that each young person needs to be formed in a family and community that recognizes first and foremost that we come from the hand of God, we return to God, and we have all sinned and are in need of the redemption offered to us in the Risen Lord. The love of God that surpasses all things is coupled with our need for forgiveness of sins, which the Lord extends to us if we open our hearts. If all we have is the love of God, there is moral laxity. On the other hand, if all you have is sinfulness, then you have authoritarian parenting. If all you have is advertising, then you have permissive parenting.

We live in a postmodern world, so let us pause for a long time before the forces of environmental and cultural conditioning envelop us and ask a few essential questions. If environmental conditioning and marketing win the day, what will those who look back on us say 100 years from now? Will they look at our age as having made a giant step forward in human progress, or as an example of early mass marketing gone astray? Will they say we made a positive difference in the world, or that we were a part of its ultimate destruction?

# CHAPTER EIGHT

# Appropriate and Inappropriate Self-Love

———◦◦◦———

*U need 2 no wat self-luv is k n not k.*

You need to know what self-love is OK and not OK.

In the last two decades, I have seen countless kids who have had every ounce of self-respect, self-worth, and dignity as children of God stolen from them. Much is written about these kids, and rightly so. They are deserving of compassion, hope, health, and healing. This eighth "dispatch from the front" goes to the very heart of how to deal with children who either love themselves too little or too much, to the detriment of themselves and others.

A good example of kids who cannot like themselves and do not love themselves are sexually abused kids who have no sense of self-worth. It seems to them their bodies do not belong to them. They belong to others, who use them for their own selfish purposes. The lack of self-love of these children needs urgent remedy.

Take 17-year-old Cynthia, who called our Hotline wanting to talk about her attempted suicide (overdosing) the day before. She was gang raped and contracted sexually transmitted diseases three months ago. Everything was reported, but the boys threatened her, so she did not press charges. Her anger is turned inward into self-hatred. Thank goodness she is willing to accept help.

For other kids coming here who have suffered much, the anger is turned not inward but outward. They only want to hurt other people. In this regard, Viktor Frankl tells a story in his classic *Man's Search for Meaning:*

> [Some of the concentration camp's survivors] could not escape the influences of the brutality which had surrounded them in camp life. Now being free, they thought they could use their freedom licentiously and ruthlessly. The only thing that had changed for them was that they were now the oppressors instead of the oppressed. . . . a friend was walking across a field with me towards a camp when suddenly we came to a field of green crops. Automatically, I avoided it, but he drew my arm through mine and dragged me through it. I stammered something about not treading down the young crops. He became annoyed, gave me an angry look and shouted: "You don't say! And hasn't enough been done to us?"

So when is self-love appropriate and when is it misguided? The wise medieval scholar, Thomas Aquinas, explained it this way. He said appropriate self-love is love of self that is ordered to the love of God and love of neighbor. It stems, he said, from love of God, who sees the person as his own beloved son or daughter, made in his own image and likeness, and called to eternal life. It follows that if we bask in the love of God, we should begin to have a growing recognition of our God-given mission — a sense that we have to develop virtues, talents, and character in order to be able to do the mission God has put us each on this earth to carry out.

So we each have to be solicitous about our health and well-being in order to carry out this mission with success. Concern for our mission also means we have to confess our sins and shortcomings in the light of God's forgiving love, because our sins and shortcomings impede our love of our brothers and sisters. What is this love of neighbor? It is doing something worthwhile for them, something truly valuable, and something even involving sacrifice on our part. To do so, we have to make sure we have enough good health, education, and moral well-being to succeed in this venture. A mother cannot love her children appropriately if she neglects her health and is sick all the time. She has to think about herself because her baby needs her.

In Thomas Aquinas' view, inappropriate self-love is not ordered to love of God and love of neighbor, but is just plain selfishness. Inappropriate self-love is shoplifting, lying about it, and then getting angry when people don't believe the lies. Inappropriate self-love is manipulating others so I get my way. Inappropriate self-love is making myself look good by putting others down. Inappropriate self-love is thoughtlessness, not seeing the needs of others — or seeing these needs but not responding to them. Inappropriate self-love is taking care of myself and no one else. Inappropriate self-love is doing nothing to stop evil from happening because it would be inconvenient.

**DISPATCH A**

Fr. Flanagan often told the story of ten-year-old Billy, who had robbed a bank in the South Bronx and who repeatedly declared to Fr. Flanagan that he was a bad boy and very proud of it. Fr. Flanagan kept telling him, "No, you are a good boy who had bad friends who taught you bad things. You are a good boy and we have good teachers here who can teach you good things." The tug of war went on for quite a while, but Fr. Flanagan's firm discipline surrounded by love won out. Billy began to take what Robert Frost called "The Road Less Traveled" and it "made all the difference." This is moving away from self-absorption.

In our own day, a popular way of looking at the difference between appropriate self-love and selfishness is to distinguish between self-donation and self-absorption. Much has been written in this regard, but it basically amounts to this. As we go through life, what is the basic flow of our person and our character? Is it a basic flow of giving of self? Or are we mostly selfish? Self-absorbed?

Do we look at the needs of others and try to respond to them? Are we considered caring, sharing people most of the time? When the times get rough, are we still caring and sharing? That is the basic flow of self-donation. If you could have seen Fr. Flanagan working every day with the boys of Boys Town, it would have dawned on you what the basic thrust of his life was. He was often ill but worked hard to get better so he could help more boys. That is true of all great moms, all great dads, all great sons, and all great daughters.

How do we help change a child who has become self-absorbed? Let me give you the example of Mercedes, who came to us from Tampa at age 14. She had been abused by her grandfather and her mom's boyfriends since age 3, and neither her mother nor her grandmother had lifted a hand to stop it. Mercedes had shuttered the windows of her heart and lived in the darkness ever since. Now, she steadfastly refused to let anyone get close to her. In her own words, "If I cannot have the love of my mother and my grandmother who have abandoned me, I will not let anyone love me."

The Scriptures say that it is God who has loved us first, not us who first loved God. That is a key to helping kids like Mercedes. I start these kids off with a simple exercise in learning how to pray; however, I needed to wait until the right time came to teach it to Mercedes.

In the midst of her self-absorption, Mercedes began to like living in the Village of Boys Town. She was now doing well in school; she had a home where there was warmth, caring, and some good, solid, strict discipline. She was feeling better about herself and getting help with the abuse issues. So it was time to act.

I asked her to spend ten minutes every day for seven days in Dowd Chapel by herself, alone, with no one else there. When she went in, she was to sit down and look up at the altar and the tabernacle, where the good Lord Himself is, and she was to simply open her arms and open her heart and say, "Lord, I will let you love me." She was to close her eyes and feel the Good Shepherd taking her in His arms like a lost lamb and taking her gently home.

She didn't like the idea but was willing to try, and slowly, it began to work. With her feeling the love of the Lord, she gradually began to feel a little better about those around her. That was a giant move forward. She was moving away from self-absorption and heading toward self-donation.

This isn't the only time I've used this technique to help a child. One night, sitting in the front pew of Dowd Chapel saying my prayers, I heard sniffles coming from the back of church. So I spoke up loudly: "Whoever is back there, please come up front. I am too tired to come look for you." Ten-year-old Freddy came up, sat down beside me, and asked, "Father, will you teach me how to pray?" At the time, I was praying the Divine Office, the official prayer of the Church, so I said, "Freddy, be quiet while I finish a little prayer here and I will show you how." Then, when I was done, I showed him the technique I had taught Mercedes, and told him to be quiet, sit there, and practice it.

I continued my prayers, only to hear him sniffling again a few minutes later. I asked him what was wrong, but he just said, "Shush, Father. Jesus is loving me."

---

**DISPATCH B**

Cecily once told me, "I see no reason why I should care for anyone other than myself." When I asked her if there was any living creature (such as a puppy or a kitten or a person) she really liked or loved, she assured me that there were none. One day, she got into a shouting match with the female supervisor and went after her with a wooden mallet. I assumed this was all on the spur of the moment. But by now, I had gained her trust, so she told me secretly, "Don't tell anyone else, but I planned that for three days." That is self-absorption.

---

That is the beginning of appropriate self-love. It is followed by letting others love you and loving them in return.

I mentioned earlier that Christopher Lasch put a spotlight on our culture's version of self-love in his 1979 book, *The Culture of Narcissism*. Lasch says the exaggerated individualism of our society is a "turn inward." It is certainly narcissistic. The self-esteem movement has moved us away from a communitarian focus and into a narcissistic self-focus. The turn inward has found fertile ground in the anti-authoritarianism of the time. Incidentally, the word *narcissism* comes from an ancient Greek myth about young Narcissus who, while walking along one day, saw himself in a lake and fell in love with the image. In one version of the story, he was so enamored with himself that he did not watch where he was going, fell in the lake, and drowned. In the other version, he was so in love with his image that he died of starvation, choosing to look at himself rather than take care of himself.

The insistence that I come first before anyone else; that I am to be admired; that there is no reason for me to admire you, or have empathy or compassion for you, except when it reflects favorably on me . . . these are all characteristics of the exaggerated individualism of our age. It is widespread and rampant. Here are three examples.

- Almost every young person is on the social networking sites My Space or Facebook, places often filled with self-centered untruths, puffery, and fanciful self-promotion. If all we write about is ourselves and exaggerate and fantasize on and on, this reinforces the notion that I do come first and that is the way it will always be. The number of kids I know who have been harmed grievously by libel and slander of other kids on My Space is legion. This is narcissism gone wild.

- The second example is text messaging. We were sitting in McDonald's having a Big Mac, and two of the kids were text messaging someone else. This is not only a violation of the canons of common courtesy, but it reinforces the notion that their individual wishes come first. It is hard to be the friend of such selfish persons, unless you are selfish yourself.

- The third example of how widespread this self-absorption or narcissism is can be seen in the world of work. Young people sometimes come to the job with the idea there is no reason to find out how things have been done in the past. After all, I am a person filled with self-esteem and good ideas. Whatever I decide to do should be applauded. This is a little exaggerated, but not much. I have seen that hundreds of times at Boys Town. I really cannot blame the young people because they are so conditioned by the toxicity of a narcissistic culture to which they have succumbed.

Narcissism moves from a personality type/character trait to a character disorder when it begets a grandiose sense of self and generates the unrealistic expectation that everyone else should feel the same way about the person involved, even though he or she has no empathy for others. In the *DSM-IV-TR* (*Diagnostic and Statistical Manual, Fourth Edition, Text Revision*), the diagnostic criteria for this mental illness are described as follows:

> A pervasive pattern of grandiosity (in fantasy or behavior), need for admiration, and lack of empathy, beginning by early adulthood and

present in a variety of contexts, as indicated by five (or more) of the following:

- Has a grandiose sense of self-importance (e.g., exaggerates achievements and talents, expects to be recognized as superior without commensurate achievements).

- Is preoccupied with fantasies of unlimited success, power, brilliance, beauty, or ideal love.

- Believes that he or she is "special" and unique and can only be understood by, or should associate with, other special or high-status people (or institutions).

- Requires excessive admiration.

- Has a sense of entitlement, i.e., unreasonable expectations of especially favorable treatment or automatic compliance with his or her expectations.

- Is interpersonally exploitative, i.e., takes advantage of others to achieve his or her own ends.

- Lacks empathy: is unwilling to recognize or identify with the feelings and needs of others.

- Is often envious of others or believes that others are envious of him or her.

- Shows arrogant, haughty behaviors or attitudes.

True narcissistic personality disorder, a major mental disorder, is not very common. What is of more concern to us is just plain garden-variety selfishness, which is very common today.

Let's see five remedies for garden-variety selfishness and see how they play out.

1) The first step forward is to realize you are selfish and to pray to God to be delivered from it. It is only with God's power that you lose your powerlessness. One of our alums, George, has been in AA for three years. The first step in AA is to admit you are powerless before drugs and alcohol, and the second step is to get in touch with a Higher Power. George said, "I knew those first two steps were true, but I never could get in touch with my Higher Power until I got down on my knees like I did as a child. And then I was in touch with the Lord and power came."

2) The second step is to learn how to receive negative feedback, to practice receiving criticism and taking it to heart. If you do not know what needs negative feedback, just ask your family or coworkers. They will be happy to tell you. While waiting at the Denver airport for a flight to Los Angeles, I noticed a family (mom, dad, and a teenage son). The dad said he would go bring back some snacks. On this return, he handed his son a bag of potato chips. The boy took one look at it and loudly said, "I don't want this s—. I want barbeque potato chips." This selfish young man needs negative feedback and right away, almost like yesterday.

3) Selfish people often have a sense of entitlement or unreasonable expectations for favorable treatment or demand automatic compliance of others. They use anger when others do not fulfill their expectations. If you are

the one getting angry, you urgently need to practice some pre-emptive self-talk to lower your expectations. Remind yourself that you must listen to others, and that you can't automatically expect others to follow your ideas because others have good ideas as well. Don't exempt yourself from the rules of common courtesy.

---

**DISPATCH C**

Nine-year-old Temperence, who is in our New Orleans shelter, has the biggest smile on her face despite having experienced many troubles in her short life. I asked her why she was smiling and she said, "I used to feel sorry for myself, but I like it here very much." Pint-sized Temperence has jumbo-sized courage. What a lesson for all of us.

---

4) A selfish person feels he or she is superior, special, and unique, and expects others to recognize this. Often, these people will associate with people of high status. They need to start spending time with people of normal status who don't seem to notice how "superior" they are. If you do that, your friends will be shocked, and the "little people" will be pleased.

I like to tell this story on myself. One day, a very prominent socialite asked me if I belonged to the country club and I said no, I did not belong to the country club, but I did belong to Sam's Club. She seemed sort of confused by my response. I wonder why?

5) Practice identifying with the feelings and needs of others. Serve meals to the homeless. Go work with Mother Teresa's Sisters of Charity. Join the St. Vincent de Paul Society in your area. It is much worth the effort. When we told Josephine, age 14, we were going to a women's shelter to serve food to these victims of physical abuse at home, she said, "I don't owe these people anything. They did nothing for me." But after several such trips, including listening to the stories of so many battered women, she said, "I like coming here. I used to feel sorry for myself. That is all changing."

Eliminating selfishness is impossible without long, daily prayer and self-denial. If you pray to be delivered from narcissism, that is a gigantic first step. If you pray often for it, the Lord will give you this gift. To begin a strong relationship with the Lord is to move away from yourself as center of everything — to move away from "my will be done" to "Thy will be done," moving to the Lord being the source of goodness and center of all.

Selfish people pray, "Listen Lord, your servant is speaking." Unselfish people pray, "Speak, Lord, your servant is listening."

# CHAPTER NINE

# A Twenty-First-Century Christian Way of Life

*U need 2 no the secret 2 private n public virtue n wat u can do 2 help.*

You need to know the secret to private and public virtue and what you can do to help.

This final "dispatch from the front" doesn't so much survey what is new in the world in the twenty-first century as show how our response as Christians to the postmodern era is to be "in the world, but not of the world" in ways quietly different and slightly countercultural. This is what we need to teach our children. Many things make us indistinguishable from our contemporaries, but there are some things that can make us distinctive. By pointing this out, we hope you will come away with a concrete plan of action for your own family, school, and church.

Let us start with a second-century view of Christians as they saw themselves. This letter, by an unknown early second-century Christian writer to Diognetus, speaks eloquently to us about the first Christians:

> Christians are indistinguishable from other men, either by nationality, language or

customs. They do not inhabit separate cities of their own, or speak a strange dialect, or follow some outlandish way of life. Their teaching is not based on reveries inspired by the curiosity of men. Unlike some other people, they champion no purely human doctrine. With regard to dress, food and manner of life in general, they follow the customs of whatever city they happen to be living in, whether it be Greek or foreign.

And yet there is something extraordinary about their lives. They live in their own countries as though they are only passing through. They play their full role as citizens, but labor under all the disabilities of aliens. Any country can be homeland, but for them their homeland, wherever it may be, is a foreign country. Like others, they marry and have children, but they do not expose them. They share their meals, but not their wives. They live in the flesh, but they are not governed by the desires of the flesh. They pass their days upon earth, but they are citizens of heaven. Obedient to the laws, they yet live on a level that transcends the law.

Christians love all men, but all men persecute them. Condemned because they are not understood, they are put to death, but raised to life again. They live in poverty, but enrich many; they are totally destitute, but possess an abundance of everything. They suffer dishonor, but that is their glory. They are defamed, but vindicated. A blessing is their answer to abuse, deference is their answer to insult. For the good they do, they receive the punishment of malefactors, but even then they rejoice as though receiving the gift of life. They are attacked by the Jews as aliens, they are persecuted by the Greeks, yet no one can explain the reason for this hatred.

To speak in general terms, we may say that the Christian is to the world what the soul is to the body. As the soul is present in every part of the body while remaining distinct from it, so Christians are found in all the cities of the world, but cannot be identified with the world. As a visible body contains the invisible soul, so Christians are seen living in the world, but their religious life remains unseen.[1]

To be true to their calling, Christians need to follow the Lord, even when it means being seen as holding a different world view — starting with how we view ourselves. In our secular world, the self is thought of as the unfettered individual in isolation. The focus is inward, not outward. We Christians need to teach our children that we begin not

---

[1] Text can be found at http://www.vatican.va/spirit/documents/spirit_20010522_diogneto_en.html.

with a sense of isolation but of belonging, of relationship, of the redemptive. So if Christians are asked how they define themselves and are asked to explain who they are and what is this thing called the "self," their answer is this: The self is not an unfettered individual in isolation. The self is relational. It is not lonely. It begins with relationships.

When someone asks, "Who are you?" the response of a Christian should first be, "I am a child of God, the Father who created me, the Son who redeemed me, and the Holy Spirit who empowered me. Blessed Mary is our mother, as is the Church, the people of God. The saints are our brothers and sisters." Then we add our unique details: "In addition, I am the son of Carl and Anne Marie Peter. I have two brothers and a sister and a vast number of uncles, aunts, and cousins."

The divine family of God the Father, Son, and Holy Spirit and the human family are what define us first and foremost. We are defined first by the relational dimensions of the human person as son/daughter, brother/sister, father/mother, nephew, grandson, and all of these. Your goal and mine is union with God and others in God. That is why God created you and me.

Through this book, we have seen something begin to occur after World War II that can best be described as a subtle shift in the definition of self — moving from the communitarian, relational, and family definition to a definition that looks inside the person as an individual, to the needs and wants of that individual. In other words, the secular world would suggest you are, first and foremost, an inner self with inner needs, an isolated person. The Gospel, on the other hand, suggests you are first and foremost a member of the divine family with God as creator, redeemer, and sanctifier with a dad and a mom, brothers, sisters, and grandparents. Our secular culture believes you are just an individual. Our religious faith starts with the belief that you are a family member. The first is lonely. The second is a matter of belonging. Our children need to know this.

How did this change occur? During the Depression and World War II, there was a great need to tough it out and to sacrifice in extraordinary ways that reinforced our Christian notion of belonging. On our better days, we stressed the good we had in common and tried, more often than not, to make an individual contribution to our family, both the human family and the divine family. God put us on earth for this purpose. We were clear about that. Heaven was our goal.

When the Depression and World War II ended and affluence arrived, this need for one another seemed less urgent, less apparent. Along with this lack of urgency came an increased impatience — perhaps even intolerance — of family dysfunction that we had chosen (or had no choice but) to overlook before. We began to stress a little more what was wrong with our families instead of what was right. After all, affluence doesn't mean that we have more needs and wants. It is the subtle shift from wanting more to expecting more . . . even from our families. So we began to see our families as less functional then they ought to be. More stress was now on what was wrong in relationships.

There was no conspiracy to ruin family ties, no cabal to orchestrate all this, but it was happening.

With the rise of affluence came a group of humanistic psychologists (as distinguished from experimental psychologists and behavioral psychologists) who had the following views (that our children may not be aware of):

1) You need to embrace the idea that self-actualization is your goal. You need to look inward instead of outward for your identity. Your emphasis should be on the internal authority of the self, not on the external authority outside yourself. Your family is a mess in some ways. It is an increasingly depressing experience to look at family relationships and define yourself that way. If your family is a mess and you look at family relations to define yourself, that will be increasingly frustrating, so look inward.

2) As you look inward, you will find yourself defining fulfillment as the realization of your potential and not, as you did in the Christian scheme, of the outward goal of loving one another, of helping one another, of worshiping the Lord, and all meeting some day in heaven.

3) If you look, you will find inside yourself a multiplicity of needs, feelings, and wants. In some sense, this multiplicity can take the place of your many dysfunctional relatives. Cater to these needs and feelings. Jung said it clearly: As you go inside yourself, you meet archetypal figures. As you develop interest in your inner self, quite appropriately, you will have less interest in your brothers, sisters, parents, and family.

Now the changes in our economy since 2008 are starting, ever so slowly, to impact this turn inward. Not long ago, *USA Today* reported that the sub-prime mortgage crisis, the crash of the housing market, and job losses are causing some family members to move in and live under the same roof, once again, as in the past. With less money available, older parents are moving back in with their grown children, due to the now prohibitive expenses of other retirement arrangements. Young people return to the family home to get established. Even siblings are starting to share apartments. The newspaper reports say many such folks find that they are growing closer as a family and learning how to live together again. They are rediscovering the riches of family life. On the other hand, the cultural elite find this an attack on their views of the self. For example, in *No More Ramen* — a sort of survival guide for tough economic times — Nicholos Aretakis is quoted as saying: "When you move in with your family you lose that sense of independence, privacy and self-esteem. You lose something of your identity." Hurray for losing that kind of identity, if the loss fosters interdependence!

Another thing that happened after World War II was that Catholics witnessed a surge of vocations. Many soldiers returning from the war had seen enough death, destruction, hatred, and revenge to long for a monastic routine of prayer and solitude. Thomas Merton's *Seven Storey Mountain* was their inspiration. Viktor Frankl's *Man's Search for Meaning* was their search, too. Faith life was identified with the interior life. After the fall of Nazism, faith life was not a search for peace and justice;

the Cold War had now begun and peace and justice seemed even further removed than before.

So when Maslow, Erikson, Rogers, and others came upon the scene, with their insistence on the centrality of the therapeutic, Christian faith in America began to wander off the proven path that Christians had taken through the centuries and often turned to the therapeutic more than to the redemptive. Of course, this was a huge loss.

Some interpreters of Vatican II made this trend formidable. Why? Vatican II told us to open ourselves to the insights of modern psychology and sociology. But these interpreters began to read Maslow, Erikson, and others *uncritically* in relation to our Christian worldview. If you start to define yourself as a bundle of internal needs, then the ascetical practices (prayer, mortification, and fasting) so essential to gaining freedom for union with God (and others in God) start to diminish in importance and even vanish. Many interpreters following Maslow, Erikson, and others were saying that certain of these ascetical Christian practices (mortification and fasting) and feelings (guilt and shame) are out of bounds and bad by definition. The notion of sin diminished and its place was taken by "errors" or "mistakes." We did not sin; we just made mistakes. The remedy for sin is repentance, but the remedy for mistakes is therapy/education. And the more mistakes, the greater need for therapy. This was a conscious attempt on the part of some humanistic psychologists to do away with the relationship with God. They even acknowledged it as such.

It is easy to see the progression, the developmental pattern, evolving. Many in America began to move away from a Christian perspective of redemption to a more humanistic, therapeutic perspective. At some point after Vatican II, the search inward — the search for identity and the need for fulfillment — began to skew the renewal of the Catholic Church in America. Catholics were told to open the windows to modern society, as there were many things we needed to be open to. But we could have been more critical, more discerning, in what was worthwhile and what was not when we opened the windows! Sand and dirt came in, together with the fresh air.

In the past, our moral lives had external rules, but now there was only internal authority, not external authority; only internal rules, not external rules, and these were the rules of developmental psychology gone astray.

Our task now, for ourselves and our children, is to recover — or rediscover, if you like — the incarnational and redemptive Christian view, where relationships take precedence over our inner selves and where one looks outside of oneself to find meaning and fulfillment. Our goal is union with God and others in God. If the pursuit of this goal makes us slightly countercultural, then so be it. We need to regain our family focus, our community focus, our church focus, and move away from an almost narcissistic self-focus in our Christian lives. The self-esteem movement hurt us more than it helped us.

Once again, it is important to note that many of the advances in developmental psychology and sociology were very, very good indeed, but not all of them. To be countercultural, we need to distinguish between the good and the bad. We need to follow St. Paul's advice: "Do not be overcome by evil, but overcome evil by doing good." Certain experiences are enormously harmful to human flourishing, to human freedom. No matter how hard we try, they will not be healing experiences.

In addition, people have discovered that simply getting in touch with one's past and naming it does not always or necessarily bring health. Christians would say that the healing comes at the point when we are able to turn this past over to God and experience true repentance, reconciliation, feelings of acceptance, and newness of life. It is the Christian who says, "Father, I have sinned against heaven and Thee." It is the secular humanist who says, "Our father has sinned against heaven and me."

The description our humanistic psychologists gave of our needs and wants is valid only as long as it remains descriptive and not prescriptive. It describes many of our inner needs and wants, but it does not give us a moral path. It is quite wrong to say the self is innocent until it has contact with others and then it is contaminated by parents, family, and social contact. That is a denial of original sin, a doctrine that teaches that the self is not wholly innocent at the start. In this new scheme of things, social justice is a matter of "sinful institutions," or "sinful structures." It is a matter of sinfulness outside ourselves. Karl Marx believed that. Lenin did, too. Communism tried that with singular lack of success. Even the hippie communes of the late 1960s and early 1970s believed it and they, too, failed miserably.

The self is not totally innocent. That was an old Pelagian view. Neither is the self totally corrupt. That was an old view found in some of St. Augustine's writings. The Church has taught clearly that the self is wounded and needs spiritual healing. And the healing cannot happen in splendid isolation. The self is capable of great virtue and, of course, great viciousness, too.

Viktor Frankl, whose book *Man's Search for Meaning* has touched the hearts of so many and sold more than twelve million copies, says it this way:

> We may learn that there are two races of men in this world, but only these two — the race of the decent man and the race of the indecent man. Both are found everywhere; they penetrate into all groups of society. No group consists entirely of decent or indecent people. In this sense, no group is of pure race — and therefore one occasionally found a decent fellow among the camp guards.[2]

The founders of the American republic insisted that we could not have a truly democratic society without self-discipline, self-denial, and private and public virtue in the service of others, paying our bills, and honoring our contracts — not lying, cheating, and stealing. If everyone only has self-interest as the highest priority, democracy will not flourish. Private and public virtue — the spirit of sacrifice for the sake of others — is important if the republic of America is to survive and prosper.

---

[2] Frankl, p. 94.

More and more people today recognize this truth about virtue as being an important component of a free democratic society. What has been forgotten for a long time but, as a result of our worldwide economic downtown, is slowly coming to our consciousness is that the need for virtue is as true in business and commerce as it is in our individual lives. When the attitude of "we can do no wrong" combines with greed, the world economy gets better only for a short time and then collapses. The world will not get better unless the greed, arrogance, lying, and cheating stop.

A healthy economic system is impossible without honesty, humility, and integrity. Adam Smith, in his *Wealth of Nations*, insisted that if everyone simply pursued their own private good (their own self-interest or selfishness), then the common economic good would be taken care of. Balderdash! Past and present history shows it doesn't work that way.

Two examples come quickly to mind.

- During a recent lunch with an executive secretary here at Boys Town, I asked her why she quit her job at a national mortgage firm three years ago to join us. She hesitated, then explained slowly, "I was tired of falsifying salary stubs for home loans."

- A few short days ago, a 21-year-old grad told an auto dealership his salary would only allow him to borrow $9,000, but he liked the $12,000 auto. "No problem," said the dealer. "We'll just use someone else's pay stubs."

Many historians think that the growth of commerce was an enormous advance over the view of the ancient conquerors. But commerce is an advance only to the degree that virtue rules there as well. If today's business men and women engage in these tactics, they have made no advances from the days of Alexander the Great, who sought great wealth by war, pillage, and plunder. Take away private and public virtue and commerce can be as rapacious and as destructive as Genghis Khan. We need to change ourselves. We cannot do it by ourselves. We need the grace of God.

In our long Christian tradition, there are two practices that make us different. The first is the practice of virtue and the second is the practice of self-denial and self-restraint.

The second-century Christian writer quoted at the beginning of this chapter quite rightly said we Christians are only slightly countercultural. We have already seen what this means for defining the self. We now see that our identity consists of being really and truly called by God and sent on a mission as we come into the world. This means we Christians need to begin with an affirmative response to God's call: "Come, follow Me." Our call echoes the call of God to Abraham and Sarah. It echoes the call of God to Samuel, whose response was, "Speak, Lord, your servant is listening." And, of course, then there was Joshua's "For me and my household, we will serve the Lord."

In the long Christian tradition, this commitment to serve the Lord has a strange name. It is called *devotion*. Devotion is described as an act of the will whereby we surrender ourselves to the service of God. It is an in-depth decision that sometimes comes gradually, sometimes quickly. The rest of the world does not notice this happening in our lives, but we notice it profoundly because our hearts are now flooded with joy.

In reflecting on this, St. Thomas suggests there are two kinds of things to notice that bring us to this dedication of our lives to God:

> The one is the consideration of God's goodness and loving kindness and this awakens love which is the proximate cause of devotion. The other consideration is our own shortcomings, on account of which we need to lean on God.[3]

It should be clear that our becoming the Lord's good servant means that we are entering into a new, profound relationship with God. The direct effect of devotion is joy. When the world sees a joyful Christian, it often calls that person simply a happy personality and nothing more. But there is so much more to it than the world can see.

Once one decides to follow the Lord, then the question arises — what does the following of the Lord entail? The Gospels unanimously respond, "Take up thy cross and follow Me." Be a good Samaritan. The Gospels tell us to feed the hungry, give drink to the thirsty, visit the sick, clothe the naked, love your neighbor as yourself. The Scriptures tell us we cannot do this by ourselves. We need

---

[3] *Summa Theologica*, II.II. Q82, Article 3.

virtue, grace under pressure, spiritual courage. And we need moral muscle that is strength.

To grow in friendship with God also requires considerable self-mastery on our part, in order to gain freedom to serve God and neighbor. Scripture is filled with admonitions in this regard. There is the story of the king who, before he does battle with an opposite king, has to sit down and figure out whether he has strength enough and forces enough to conquer . . . and the person who wants to build a house and has to figure if he has the resources to do so . . . and, at the end of the Sermon on the Mount is the fool who built his house on sand; the winds and storms came, and his house was washed away and collapsed. What a fall it was!

It is through repeated acts of virtue, with works of charity and self-denial, that hope grows in our lives. Real hope is nothing more and nothing less than the deep-seated confidence that things will work out, developed by daily trusting in God over long periods of time. Hope is the profound realization that God is in charge, and that we will make it through with trust in Him. In other words, as we feed the hungry; give drink to the thirsty; deny ourselves; say no to our anger, hatred, revenge, laziness, and just plain selfishness; and live through rocky times, hope springs up, grows strong, and energizes our emotional and spiritual lives.

If we give up our traditional, ascetical practices (whose goal is to give us freedom to serve the Lord), our devotion to God slowly but surely grows cold. What we must do, to make a real difference in our lives and the lives of our children, is to help our children integrate our ancient practices with the best insights of postmodern psychology so that we may be in the world, but not of the world.

# Epilogue

We live in hopeful times. The winds of change are blowing. The age of opulence is over.

We are turning more and more to one another as family becomes increasingly important. These winds of change give us just the opportunity we need to refashion our families, schools, and communities.

We know what works so that love wins out, so that we restore to health more of our children, more of our families, more of our schools, more of our churches.

For love to win out, we — and our children — will need courage to be slightly unconventional, slightly countercultural. Alessandro Manzoni, in his classic novel *The Betrothed*, tells the story of a young couple in the village who want to get married and approach the priest to officiate. However, the nobleman who controls everything in the village has an eye for the girl and threatens the priest with death if he performs the marriage. The priest yields to the nobleman's wishes, but when the story reaches the ears of his bishop, Cardinal Federigo Borromeo, the cardinal chastises him for his cowardice. The priest excuses himself by saying, "One cannot give oneself courage."

But the Cardinal persists:

> "How is it that you do not remember . . . that there is One who will infallibly bestow

it upon you, when you ask Him? Think you all the millions of martyrs naturally possessed courage? that they naturally held life in contempt? . . . All possessed courage because courage was necessary, and they relied upon God . . . But a holy and noble fear for others, for your children . . . . this would have incited — constrained you to think and do all you could to avert the dangers that threatened them [the young couple]."[1]

Pray for courage, my dear reader.

Pray for courage.

And I know from experience — after all these years on the front — that if you pray for it, God will give it to you.

---

[1] *I Promessi Sposi* (*The Betrothed*), pp. 436-37.

# *Notes*

*Notes*

# Notes